THE
WHERE
TO EAT®
GUIDE

sizzle
&buzz

The Where To Eat Guide & Associates, Inc.
PO Box 6224
Bend, OR 97708

ISBN 978-0-9910413-0-5

For information about special sales, please contact
The Where to Eat Guide & Associates, Inc. at 877-503-1266 or info@theEatGuide.com.

Manufactured in the United States of America

4 9 10 6 7 8 5 3 2 1

www.theeatguide.com

sizzle&buzz

written by Sarah Daily

with John Herbik and Dana Bartus

Where To Eat Guide & Associates, Inc.

TABLE OF CONTENTS

FOREWORD

 I was a hungry kid. I grew up one of six children in Cleveland, Ohio. My mother worked three jobs to try to support us the best she could. We were on welfare. We were one of the families that got food baskets on Thanksgiving and Christmas from our church. If Mom heard one of us say we were hungry at night it was time for bed.

Last year, the producers of *Food, Inc.* released *A Place at the Table*, a film documenting the modern hunger crisis in America. While watching it, I recognized myself. It left me inspired to move on this project that would benefit people in need in our local communities. With more than 240 restaurants in our three Pacific Northwest magazines, I had a phenomenal pool of resources right at my fingertips. And trust me, it is by no mistake that 90 percent of the restaurants we work with are locally owned and operated. Even the chains we have chosen to represent are locally owned and set themselves apart from their competitors. The restaurateurs and chefs represented by The Where to Eat Guide & Associates, Inc. devote their lives to their work. These people are very talented, and it shows. It was a no-brainer for me to leverage their skills to benefit charity.

The result is *Sizzle & Buzz: What's Cookin' in the Region's Hottest Restaurants*. A portion of the proceeds from this book will go directly to the Portland Police Bureau's Sunshine Division, Operation Sack Lunch in Seattle, and the Hunger Prevention Coalition of Central Oregon. Not only do these organizations help fill empty plates, but they also work to increase the nutritional value of the food they provide every single day.

The bonus? Connecting you with stories and recipes from some of the region's best restaurants—the chefs and owners we are fortunate enough to work with every day in our magazines. Read on. Cook your heart out. Learn. Visit a new restaurant or be reminded of an old favorite. Remember to taste these dishes at each restaurant to see how your version compares.

John Herbik, The Where to Eat Guide, Founder & President

INTRODUCTION

This book is dedicated to the chefs and restaurateurs who took a leap of faith and followed their passion—a passion whose main goal is to bring the rest of us great comfort, nourishment and joy.

If you think about the most important moments in life, the most memorable, the ones you met with great zeal and celebration, they likely occurred in a restaurant. Even the unforeseen magical moments of happenstance over a cup of coffee, a cocktail, a shared meal with new friends—if you think about these moments, they too likely happened at a table that someone else set for you.

Despite their own personal expense, exhaustion and oftentimes fear, the chefs and owners profiled in this book fill our communities with something very important. When we eat the food, the closely held culinary artwork of others in a common, public place, something magical happens. We notice each other. We hear each other's voices. We make eye contact and exchange pleasantries. We eat the same dishes. We bond over flavor and aroma and experience. And then we come back and do it all over again.

This is what *Sizzle and Buzz: What's Cookin' in the Region's Hottest Restaurants* is all about. Restaurants are about food, of course. But they are also a destination for the best stories in life. We have chosen to share recipes and stories from the individuals who have created the environments that allow us to celebrate so well. They are stories of hard work and dedication. They are stories of flavor and expertise and experiment. They are stories of cities and sustainability and ingredients. They are stories of local businesses that were built to deliver the most primal of all human needs—nourishment and connection.

We offer great thanks to every restaurant that graciously participated and supplied us with recipes for this book. They are a beautiful reflection of diners' favorite dishes in Portland, Seattle and Bend. We also thank them for sharing the details of their lives and days.

To the reader, we encourage you to try these recipes at home and recreate something special at your own table. We also encourage you to support these chefs and owners, who can only be described as denizens of local cuisine, culture and community. Their passion is as flavorful as their best dish.

SIZZLE & BUZZ

THE WHERE TO EAT GUIDE

PORTLAND

In 2004, *Food & Wine Magazine* named Portland's Scott Dolich as the Best New Chef. This was a big moment for Portland. Chefs around the country, including a few profiled in this book, looked at the upper-left-hand corner of the US map and, for the first time, thought about Portland as a potential professional culinary destination.

On the cusp. Affordable. Laid back. Eclectic. Rough-and-tumble. These were some of the descriptors used for a city that was on its way to being the next big thing in the food world. If this was a description that fit your chef style in 2004, you were thinking about heading to Portland.

Nine years later, Portland has made a major mark with brilliant coverage in national media, book deals for several chefs, cookbook launches, James Beard awards, and now an impressively growing list of Best New Chefs by *Food & Wine Magazine*.

Perhaps this success is because of the flair and rules-be-damned attitude that symbolize the overall spirit of this city. Perhaps it is because of the culture of community that bonds each unique neighborhood. Perhaps it is because of the camaraderie between restaurants and purveyors that showcase an interconnected community of gourmands whose sum is greater than its individual parts.

Or, if we get to the heart of it, maybe it has more to do with the strength of will people have in this town. The ability to be themselves and propel forward past others' prescribed mythologies of what this challenging profession should look like. In Portland, you can wear a t-shirt while preparing a meticulous and beautiful piece of foie gras. In Portland, tattoos needn't be covered for want of a neat, clean image. In Portland, you can let your ideas percolate and grow organically. In Portland, you can be yourself. This forward-moving scene has allowed some of the country's most creative chefs to flourish.

Besides the flair and personality that underlies the burgeoning cuisine in this city, the fact that Portland is surrounded by some of the most lush and well-producing lands in the country is a big part of the story. Mushroom foragers, wine makers, artisan cheese producers and heirloom farmers drop off the absolute best, local products to restaurant doorsteps every day. Menus across the city are reminiscent of bucolic days and read like an homage to the farmer, cheese maker, and butcher.

Great beauty can be found in the neighborhood restaurants where diners find a second home amongst friends, warm fireplaces, good drink, community tables, and serious comfort from the dark and dreary days. This is where Portland really shines, even through the rain. The unpretentious spirit of compatriots joining together at a table—this is what Portland, and thus its restaurant scene, is really all about.

LITTLE BIRD BISTRO

THERE IS A certain lively clamor that defines a Parisian bistro. You know it when you experience it. Clinking dishes, bouncing voices, a bubbly energy that travels around tables and across walls. A liveliness that bursts through the kitchen door as it swings open and closed. A tinkering bell that rings with incoming guests. A moment of connection that occurs between strangers placed side-by-side.

Little Bird Bistro has recreated this spirit in the middle of downtown Portland, and what's more, the menu is full of personality and simplistic concepts that draw in guests from all over the city for lunch and dinner during the week, and for dinner on the weekends.

The second project of rock-star trio Gabriel Rucker, Andrew Fortgang and Erik Van Kley, Little Bird Bistro has often been referred to as the younger sibling to Le Pigeon, Gabriel's highly acclaimed restaurant on East Burnside.

But to be accurate, this bistro, named by the *Oregonian* as the 2012 Restaurant of the Year, has emerged with wings that are more mature and refined than those of its 'older' sibling. This is in large part thanks to Erik, once Gabriel's sous chef at Le Pigeon and now chef de cuisine at Little Bird.

"Geographically, now that I'm on the other side of the river from Gabriel, I've been forced to start cooking for myself," said Erik.

Erik first met Gabriel in the kitchen of the Gotham Tavern where Erik was a line cook and Gabriel was a sous chef. Erik says they weren't friends right off the bat. "Gabe was younger and substantially more talented than I was. I was almost a little intimidated by him. We actually started stealing moves from one another at one point," said Erik.

He recalls a conversation with his mother when he told her that a certain chef he'd met at Gotham was most definitely on the road to becoming a star. "I had no idea at the time he was going to be so big," said Erik.

And as Erik often says, their relationship since the days at Gotham is history.

Erik's style at Little Bird is simple and tasteful in the most beautiful ways. Chicken Fried Trout with gribiche, fine herbs, radishes and pickled carrots is a dish that is so gorgeous in presentation and color, you can't imagine what its simple genius will taste like until you begin to poke apart its colorful array. But it is the Cassoulet of Duck Leg with pork belly, sausage and white

> *Learn to hold a knife properly and practice with it. You need a sharp knife, but it is not necessary to have a fancy knife.*
>
> —Chef Erik Van Kley

beans that exemplifies this chef's spirit and his overarching rule of Little Bird's cuisine—that each dish should hold three components that together pack a punch and encourage interactive dining.

"If I can really punch them in the head with a pork chop, a compote and a sauce, as long as I get a French dish out of it, then I did my job," said Erik.

Erik has been packing culinary punches for most of his life. He started out in the restaurant business as a scrappy 17-year-old dishwasher in Grand Rapids, Michigan. Attracted to the cooks' energy in a restaurant called Rose's,

he worked his way out of the dish-pit and onto the line where a moment of revelation came in the simple, well-executed flavors of a macaroni and cheese gratin.

"I was lured by the cooks. They played in bands. They had tattoos. There was this whole idol factor. I wanted desperately to know what they were doing," said Erik.

For anyone that knows a bit about Erik and his Portland compatriot Gabe, you can't help but see a full-fledged story. Now, we think it's pretty safe to say that there is more than one teenager in the world looking at the tattooed arms and accolades of this chef and thinking, I want to do that.

BEETS WITH GOAT CREAM CITRUS VINAIGRETTE

Photos David Reamer

BEETS

2½ lbs whole beets
½ orange, quartered
¾ cup white wine
1 Tbs extra virgin olive oil
1 bay leaf
½ cinnamon stick
Salt

• Toss all ingredients on a sheet pan, cover, and roast in a 375° oven. • Check beets after about 1 hour. When fork tender, they are done. • Set aside to cool. • When cool, peel and dice beets then dress with Citrus Vinaigrette.

CITRUS VINAIGRETTE

½ cup orange juice, reduced by 3/4
1 Tbs champagne vinegar
½ medium sized shallot, brunoise
Pinch espelette powder
3 Tbs blended oil
1 Tbs hazelnut oil
Salt

• Place orange juice in a pan and heat gently until reduced by 3/4 and then cool. • Meanwhile, macerate shallots in champagne vinegar. • Mix cooled juice, vinegar and shallots, and espelette powder. • Slowly add oils to emulsify. • Season with a touch of salt.

GOAT CREAM

½ cup crème fraiche
1 oz goat cheese, by weight
1 oz buttermilk, by volume
Salt

• Place all ingredients in a food processor and mix until smooth.
• Set aside.

HAZELNUTS

½ qt roasted hazelnuts (Little Bird loves Freddy Guys Hazelnuts, but you can also roast and peel at home)
1 Tbs sugar
8 Tbs butter
¼ tsp espelette powder
Dried zest of 1/2 orange

• Melt sugar in pan, add butter and stir to combine. • Add hazelnuts, espelette powder and dried zest. • Toss to combine. • Season with salt, allow to cool, and then pulse in food processor.

TO SERVE

• On 12" chilled round plate, pool goat cream. • Drizzle vinaigrette around the edge. • Build dressed beets and top with several candied hazelnuts. • Top with a few mizuna and/or mache leaves dressed in Citrus Vinaigrette, salt and lemon juice.

• Drizzle very top of salad with a bit of good quality extra virgin olive oil and top with a few chopped chives.

MUCCA OSTERIA

IF YOU WERE PAYING CLOSE
attention to the streets of downtown Portland in the spring of 2011, you might have noticed a young Roman cyclist pedaling with a passion from building to building. Among the swaths of bike commuters that pace this city, there was something special about this man and his daily ride.

He was on a search, by bike, for the space that would hold his greatest lifelong dream: An authentic Italian Osteria.

"We had no budget, not much money. I bicycled from place to place, looking, looking, I was looking for my restaurant," said Simone Savaiano, chef-owner of Mucca Osteria.

Simone found his restaurant on SW Morrison—a tall, airy, brick-walled space that would come to be Mucca Osteria.

Osteria, derived from the Italian word "oste," is a place that, during the Middle Ages, refueled explorers and traders with warmth, food and a relaxing atmosphere. Today, Italians frequent an osteria to enjoy small, refined menus, good wine, and warm hospitality.

Mucca Osteria reflects this idea in beautiful fashion. Entering Mucca is like taking a step into Italy, into those places where Simone was taught the importance of the most fundamental ingredients of Italian cuisine. Places like the deli in Tuscany he opened at the age of 24 with his mother and father, and his "second little place" where he grew, little by little, a passion for cooking and wine.

Now, at Mucca, the bread and pasta are made in-house every day. All of the essential ingredients, the extra virgin olive oil, the flour, and the cheeses, are all carefully hand-selected, and in fact, even the yeast for the bread is made naturally in the restaurant. Using fermented raisins, Mucca is able to produce its own yeast that gives their breads a unique, complex flavor. The pasta is made with a very traditional recipe using organic flour from local grains, egg yolks and not a drop of water.

Beyond pasta there is risotto, Pollo al Marsala with Draper Valley chicken, Marsala wine sauce, celery root purée, and brussels sprout, Coniglio Stufato con Prugne Secche with stewed rabbit from Nicky's Farm, prunes, spinach and potato, and fresh, seasonal fish with daily preparations. There is also a beautiful antipasti selection at both lunch and dinner.

Simone, also a sommelier, created an extensive wine list that is strictly Italian. In a region where American wines are abundant, Simone decided to focus only on Italian varietals to stay true to the authentic experience.

"The wine makes fifty percent of the experience. If it is not Italian, it will change the way you feel," said Simone.

Simone sums up his thoughts on the restaurant business with words that could be translated to life, to love, to risotto: "It's like a relationship with someone you love. Sometimes it's tough but you keep doing it."

It is worth noting that Simone still has that bike. Once in a while you might find him on a ride to pick up groceries, but with how busy Mucca Osteria is these days, it is a rare occasion.

> *It's like a relationship with someone you love. Sometimes it's tough but you keep doing it.*
>
> —Simone Savaiano, chef-owner

The Secret

Risotto can be simple to make, you will just need to follow some advice. The veggie stock for example, you can make your own by using fresh ingredients, even just simple carrots, celery and onions. Place them in a large stockpot with cold water, bring it to boil and then reduce the heat and keep it there for 30 minutes. In Italy we say, "All make the broth." That means that you can use pretty much everything, all the veggie scrap that you have in the house for doing this, but be careful, some colorful one can give prevalence with their color.

Risotto speck, radicchio and Taleggio cheese is a classic one, the bitterness of radicchio contrasts the sweetness of the Taleggio, the speck will give a nice smoky finish. Love it and have fun in the kitchen, this is the secret.

—Simone Savaiano, chef-owner

RISOTTO CON SPECK, RADICCHIO E TALEGGIO

(Serves 2)

½ cup Carnaroli rice
5-6 leaves of radicchio Trevigiano
⅓ cup speck (an Italian cured, smoked meat)
¼ cup Taleggio cheese
1⅔ cup veggie stock
2 shallots
2 Tbs Parmigiano Reggiano
2 Tbs butter
1 Tbs extra virgin olive oil
White wine
Salt, pepper and balsamic vinegar reduction to taste

• Finely chop the shallots, cut the radicchio into strips and dice the speck.
• Sautée all in a small pot with the olive oil for about two minutes.

• Add rice with a pinch of salt, toasting it at high heat for one minute while stirring.

• Deglaze with white wine, let evaporate while continuing to stir.

• Start to add the stock and stir frequently, when stock has been absorbed add more until rice is cooked al dente. This will take about 15 minutes, however check directions from the rice brand to be sure.

• At this point the risotto is not creamy, but more wet. • Add the butter and the Taleggio, stirring for one minute then remove it from the heat. It will need to rest for one minute, covered.

• Add the Parmigiano* and stir some more.

*Before adding the Parmigiano, the risotto should still be a little loose because the butter and Taleggio are just melting. The Parmigiano will give thickness to the risotto and will make it creamy. If before adding, the risotto appears too dry and thick, adjust it by adding a little stock or hot water. Remember that the risotto will get denser by cooling down, so be confident while searching for the right consistency. The risotto is a very manageable dish, if toasted right it will be hard to overcook.

• Serve as you like, on a plate or bowl.
• Add more Parmigiano on top, fresh ground black pepper and salt to taste.
• Drizzle some balsamic reduction, or not, as you please.

COCOTTE

COCOTTE CHEF AND OWNER

Kat LeSueur lovingly recalls her childhood trips around the world with her mother and brother. France, Marrakesh, Casa Blanca. She was the fortunate daughter of a mother who loved to travel and celebrate and eat.

But one of her most endearing memories from this period is of herself, at age seven, wearing a pink beret outside of the Louvre in Paris. Her mother and brother were romping around while she was focused on one very important thing—a roast beef baguette smeared with butter.

"I think I ate the whole thing," laughs Kat.

She also remembers the butter and sugar crepes purchased from Parisian carts, and then the contrasting yet familiar flavors that appeared when the family ventured to Morocco. Food, whether it was through travel or grand dinner parties and family holiday celebrations, has always been a central part of Kat's life, and one that she grew to focus on with as much diligence as that first experience with a French baguette.

So if we told you that she left behind a career in psychology to pursue a culinary degree, you'd believe it,

right? If you heard she learned the brilliance of French fundamentals and translation from Nathan Bates at Lucy's Table in Portland, you'd agree that that makes sense, right? If we mentioned she opened her first restaurant, a charming French bistro in NE Portland, at the age of 25, you'd believe it, right? Wait…25?

Yes, at just 25 years old, Kat drew up a business plan that would give birth to her very first restaurant. She called it Cocotte.

"I think going to culinary school sparked a drive. I'd

Photos this page David Lanthan Reamer

never done anything that I was so passionate about," said Kat.

Now, through her charming kitchen, lined with wooden shelves housing white bistro-style plates and bulbous wine glasses, guests can peek through a small window into her soul. And that soul, full of focus that propelled her through culinary school, is turning out comforting, classic, old world dishes that pull from the very best of Northwest flavor and ingredient.

> *The biggest thing is mise en place, whether your recipe is easy or complex. Read the recipe at least once, fully. Then think about it. Then get your mise en place ready. That's what it's all about.*
>
> —Kat LeSueur,
> chef and owner

The word Cocotte has a variety of meanings— hen, honey, dish, chick or harlot—but it is the Poulet en Cocotte that epitomizes this restaurant's namesake. This dish, born from the milk-fed hens of Payne Family Farm, is a half-bird preparation, a pan-roasted breast and confit leg, served with farro risotto with seasonal produce, chicken demi-glace and a slow-poached egg. It's spectacular to say the least, and it's best if you order it the moment you sit down at Cocotte because they often sell out early.

Beyond the cozy richness of the Poulet en Cocotte, you will find a well-versed story of seafood. Black cod that is full of perfect texture and buttery velvet goodness. Small river salmon that in the summer sings through the restaurant with a song of local waters. Oregon albacore tuna and fried crispy sardines that melts Kat's seafood-loving heart. This is where she excels as her most authentic self and chef, and in a city that is often berated for its lack of well-executed seafood, this passion for "la mer" is welcomed and applauded.

But at the heart, the passion of Cocotte lies in its simplicity and successful translation of French bistro in Portland.

"French food translates to everything. There's a sensibility. When you have these fundamentals—you can translate it to everything," said Kat.

This winter, look for translations of in-season flavors like pomegranate, delicata squash and apples. Add in the cozy corner setting, fresh roses, botanical prints, French doors, and warm woods, and Cocotte is surely the place to go to find the comfort that only the French know how to offer.

What is Fond?

You'll see the word "fond" in Cocotte's recipe for Chicken Liver Mousse. The word comes from the French word for "bottom," and in culinary terms refers to the roasty little bits leftover in the bottom of the pan after searing meat and/or vegetables. Otherwise known as magic and should be deglazed with liquid to release flavor.

CHICKEN LIVER MOUSSE

(Serves 6 as a snack or shared appetizer)

This is a signature dish at Cocotte and is very easy to make. The recipe is adapted from a multitude of classic, basic liver mousse recipes and techniques. You can play with it and adjust the flavor by switching the liquor (wine and cognac both work well), omitting the bacon, or adding something like 1/2 an apple, chopped, which would be sautéed along with the shallot.

1   lb chicken livers, rinsed and patted dry
2   strips of bacon (whatever flavor and brand you prefer), cut into lardons
1   lb unsalted butter, cubed and room temperature
¼   cup cold heavy cream
1   large shallot thinly sliced
¼   cup Calvados (an apple brandy from the French region of Lower Normandy)
Salt and pepper to taste
Splash of sherry vinegar to finish

• Heat a large skillet over high heat and add just enough oil to coat. • Season the rinsed and dried livers with salt and pepper.

• Add the livers to the skillet and reduce heat to medium. • Leave the livers until they get a nice brown crust rendered, then flip them and immediately remove from the skillet.

• Add more oil to the skillet as needed and sauté the shallot and bacon until lightly caramelized. • Add the Calvados to deglaze and, using a wooden spoon,

scrape the fond off the bottom of the pan. • Transfer the shallots, bacon and reduced cognac to a blender or food processor.
• Add the livers.

• Purée the shallots and livers together and add the butter, piece by piece, allowing each to incorporate before adding more.

• When the butter is fully incorporated, add the cream and finish with a splash of sherry vinegar (apple cider vinegar works well too).

• Taste and adjust seasoning as needed.

• Pass the purée through a fine mesh seive or chinoise. • Pour the strained mousse into a serving dish and chill in the fridge to set. • Chill at least three hours. • Pull the mousse from the fridge and allow it to temper about half an hour before serving. • Serve with toast points or fresh bread, pickled onions, and a fruity component like a berry or apple jam.

BOKE BOWL

⛏ SLURP-SLURP. THIS IS SOMETHING
you'll hear a lot of when you visit Boke Bowl in
Portland's Central Eastside Industrial District.

Whether it's a 5-year-old little girl or a 35-year-old
professional unapologetically devouring the handmade
ramen noodles and brilliantly slow-simmered dashis whose
aromas waft through the space like a genie out of the bottle,
one thing is for sure—slurping is welcomed, applauded, and
as some ramen-loving maniacs say, an absolute necessity.

Where did this extreme slurp-ability come from? It
came from a chef with a bowl and an idea.

"Very rarely in life do you have a vision," said Boke Bowl
chef and co-owner Patrick Fleming.

But on an otherwise nondescript day, he saw it: Asian
comfort food fueled by pop-up events, blogs and social
media buzz.

Photos Tim Parsons

The Magic of Miso Paste

*Miso paste is fermented soybean that is salty, sweet
and smoky all in one. Mix miso with water and soak
tofu in it overnight before grilling. Or throw some into
a soup for an easy way to add depth and seasoning.*

—Chef Patrick Fleming

When he asked longtime pals Brannon Riceci and Tim
Parsons to sample the ramen recipes he'd been toying with at
home, the trio agreed that the concept could work.

Their first pop-up was held just a few months later
and looked more like a campsite than a proper ramen shop.
About 50 people turned out on a sickleningly hot day to the
sight of Chef Fleming cooking in a mobile unit that housed
camp stoves and just a bit of shade from the blistering
heat. The lack of finesse in the space was quickly forgotten
because of what was served — a ramen like nothing
Portland had seen before. The Boke Bowl concept gained
press and Facebook cred, and two months later when they
popped-up again, about 200 people waited in the rain to get
their hands on a steaming bowl of goodness.

From there, the pop-ups just kept getting bigger and
better and by Black Friday in 2011, just a little over a year
after their original pop-up, Boke Bowl opened as a brick-

and-mortar version of itself complete with sleek design, refined recipes, and a grassroots following that had already professed their love and addiction.

"It was pretty exciting to say the least," said Chef Fleming.

And the slurp continues. Now when you visit Boke Bowl you will find four versions of ramen—Pork with slow-smoked pulled pork, Seafood Miso with olive oil poached shrimp, Caramelized Fennel (vegetarian) with Japanese eggplant and seasonal rice cake, and the Chef Seasonal, which is a rotating item based on chef's whim, such as Rabbit Three Ways with rabbit confit and rabbit meatballs in a rabbit dashi. Add on a slow-poached egg or cornmeal crusted oysters or buttermilk fried chicken and you have all the elements of a uniquely Northwest bowl of ramen.

While the slurp is most definitely the heart of the Boke Bowl experience, be prepared to use your chopsticks for steam buns and your teeth for the epic crunch of fried chicken and house-made pickles. Also be prepared for the house-brined and smoked tofu to completely blow you away. Chef Fleming treats his fresh tofu just like he treats his fried chicken—a brine, followed by cold smoking, followed by frying. It leads to an absolutely beautiful result that thrills carnivores just as much as it does vegetarians.

The dashis, the steam buns, the noodles, the fried chicken, the miso butterscotch Twinkies (yes, Twinkies)—these cult-followed components all help to write the Boke Bowl story, which really, at its heart, is about a one-pot-meal-loving guy from Louisiana who had a vision and 20 years of experience to back it up.

"Ultimately, I want to make a lot of people happy and express myself. It's that simple," said Chef Fleming.

Judging by the hordes of slurp-happy Boke Bowl fans, Portland might just be big enough to have another Boke Bowl. And as they say, that story is to be continued.

BRUSSELS SPROUT AND CAULIFLOWER SALAD

(Serves 4)

- 8 oz brussels sprouts, peeled outer layer and halved (reserve leaves)
- 8 oz cauliflower florets
- 4 oz olive oil
- 1 tsp kosher salt
- 1 orange, segmented (preferably blood orange or cara cara)
- 2 oz Fish Sauce Vinaigrette (recipe follows)

• Place brussels sprout halves and cauliflower florets in two separate bowls.
• Toss each bowl with 2 oz of olive oil and ½ tsp salt.
• Roast cauliflower and brussels sprouts on separate sheet pans at 400° for 15-20 minutes until golden brown stirring after 10 minutes.

• Meanwhile, blanch brussels sprout leaves for 30 seconds in boiling salted water and shock in ice bath. • Drain on paper towel.
• Toss warm roasted cauliflower, brussels sprouts, blanched leaves, orange segments and vinaigrette in bowl.
• Separate amongst 4 plates or serve on large platter.

FOR THE FISH SAUCE VINAIGRETTE
(Yield approx. 8 oz)

- ½ cup fish sauce
- ¼ cup water
- ¼ cup rice vinegar
- 3 limes, juiced
- ¼ cup sugar
- 2 cloves garlic, minced
- 1 Thai or serrano chile minced

• Whisk together in bowl. This will last for 4 weeks in fridge.

TABLA MEDITERRANEAN BISTRO

THE FACT THAT CHEF- owner Adam Berger's nine-year-old daughter can make his handmade pasta recipe from start to finish without a bit of help says a lot about Adam – as a chef, as a father, as a pasta maker.

For Adam, food is all about family and good ingredients. Tabla, his Italian restaurant on Portland's east side, is the perfect reflection of this philosophy, as is Lilly, his pasta protégé and daughter.

"I'm happiest when I'm cooking, especially pasta," said Adam.

This is a very good thing for Tabla guests that enjoy the unique flavor of his pastas. His technique borrows from the traditional Piedmontese egg noodle, which calls for seventeen yolks per pound of flour. Shepherd's grain flour, farm fresh eggs and semolina come together to create the simple, luscious style of Northern Italy.

Photos Ryan Ribary

Available as half or full plates, the pasta is clearly a signature of the Tabla menu. Cavatelli with a traditional beef and pork Bolognese. Spaghetti Carbonara with pancetta, eggs and Parmigiano Reggiano. Tabla Ravioli with chard,

ricotta, poached farm egg and poppy seed butter. And perhaps the most simple, Tajarin, with truffle butter and Parmigiano Reggiano.

If you have a gluten sensitivity, Tabla has an excellent gluten-free pasta. This pasta, as well as the traditional wheat pasta, is available by the pound to go which means you can purchase fresh, beautiful pasta to finish at home. Perfect for dinner parties, holidays and quick weeknight meals.

There is, of course, more to Tabla than pasta. Risotto, Duck Confit, Coho Salmon and Calabrian Style Grilled Pork Ribs round out the menu, which is pleasantly affordable. Charcuterie is also available with meats from Fino in Fondo, Fra'Mani and Olympic Provisions. House-made gelato and sorbetto as well as chocolate cake and panna cotta are the perfect finish to a meal at Tabla.

So, what is a Jewish guy from New Jersey doing running a traditional Italian restaurant? Adam's inspiration started long ago, when he found himself touring the Italian countryside and – serendipitously some would say – several of its world-renowned trattorias.

He was in culinary school in Arizona. One day a tiny piece of paper on the job board called out to him "Come to Italy!" It was a study and apprentice trip, where he would learn the gospel of Italian cooking and then come home to spread it. He spent time at a culinary school in Barolo. He worked at Ristorante all' Enoteca, a restaurant between Alba

Pasta, Pasta

Don't be afraid to make pasta at home. It's fun. It's easy. It's great to do with the kids!

—Adam Berger, chef and owner

and Torino, where he learned to make pasta, an experience that Adam says "changed my life."

As the apprentice program promised, Adam returned home to spread the gospel – the gospel of Piedmontese pasta, you might say.

These days you'll find Adam in his kitchen at Tabla, often with Lilly or one of his other two children. This restaurant is filled with familiar faces that, along with his longstanding staff and community of regulars, make Tabla a special place to come home to.

TABLA RAVIOLI

(Serves 4)

This recipe appears difficult, but is quite easy to execute. As of 2013, Tabla estimates that they have made 40,000 of their signature ravioli, all made to order.

You will need:

Pastry bag with a large tip
Pastry cutter wheel or a pairing knife
Large slotted spoon
2 feet of work space

PASTA

• *If you make your own*, roll it on the thinnest setting on your pasta machine.
• *If store bought*, ask for the thinnest sheets. You only need about 4 feet of pasta.

• Cut the pasta into 6" rounds. You can use a pasta wheel or just a small knife. At Tabla, they use a round container as a template. • Lightly flour the rounds and cover with plastic wrap or a towel.

FILLING

½	bunch of chard, leaves torn off stem
1	cup good whole milk ricotta
¼	cup of grated Parmigiano Reggiano cheese
	Salt and pepper to taste
4	eggs, separated

TOPPING

½	lb grated Parmigiano Reggiano or Grana Padano cheese
1	Tbs poppy seeds
½	stick of melted butter

• Fill a medium sized pot halfway with water and add 2 Tbs kosher salt.
• When it comes to a boil, add the chard leaves and stir. • Let it cook 3 minutes.
• While it is cooking, make an ice bath by adding a handful of ice cubes to a quart of water in a large bowl. • Drain the chard and place in ice bath.

• When cool, remove chard and squeeze out as much water as possible. The drier the chard, the better the filling will be.
• Chop finely. • Mix the chopped chard, ricotta and Parmigiano Reggiano in a bowl with a spatula or wooden spoon.
• Add salt and pepper to taste. • Place the filling in a pastry bag.

• Bring a large sauté pan or shallow pot of water to a boil. • Add enough salt to taste like the ocean.

• Lay all 8 rounds of pasta on your work surface. • Pipe a ring of filling on 4 rounds, leaving a 1" rim. • Place an egg yolk in the center of each ravioli. • Using the whites as "glue," use your finger or a pastry brush to brush the other 4 rounds. • Carefully place the brushed rounds over the filled rounds, using your fingers to seal the edges.

• Get your big slotted spoon, 4 warm plates, melted butter, grated Parmigiano Reggiano and poppy seeds ready.
• Place the 4 ravioli in the pot and cook for 2 minutes. • Remove carefully, letting the water drain away from each ravioli.
• Place on the warm plates, drizzle with a tsp of butter, sprinkle cheese on top and then a sprinkling of poppy seeds.
• Serve immediately.

WILDWOOD

WHEN THE FINAL SHIPMENT OF the season's prized local produce rolled into Wildwood from Viridian Farms, Chef Dustin Clark embarked on a rather massive preserve-the-season pantry project.

1,500 pounds of San Marzano tomatoes for canning. 400 pounds of Calabrian peppers for pickling.

His team gathered for a processing party of sorts. Peeling that many tomatoes requires a certain level of gusto, and as many free hands as you can get. Peeling and processing, spicing and seasoning, all in an effort to capture the very best flavor of vine-ripened fruit—it is a labor of love that only a true devotee of local lands and harvests can understand.

Come January, Wildwood guests will understand. When they get a familiar burst of brightness in a soup or sauce, a delicious tease of summer flavor in the dead of winter, they will relish it. And come June, when the first hothouse heirloom begins to plump up and green on a sturdy new vine, Chef Clark will hoard that final jar or two from the season prior like his life depends on it.

"Portland is so abundant in its produce, but the season is fleeting and quick," said Chef Clark.

That's why, for the last 11 years, Wildwood has been preserving the very best of the season.

And so it goes without saying that Wildwood's dedication to fresh, seasonal produce isn't just a label or trendy tagline. The complexity of their dishes comes directly from that depth of flavor that only can be found by sourcing the best in local ingredients, many of which are found within miles of the restaurant.

> *I cook the way I feel that day. Hopefully I'm in a good mood!*
> —Chef Dustin Clark

Since joining the Wildwood team as sous chef in 1998, Chef Clark has adhered to and elevated the restaurant's main concept: Source the finest local ingredients, know your farmers, make lasting relationships, and create a cuisine that is more detailed than the final plate. This can be seen in the way he plays with the now "simplex" New American style of Wildwood's cuisine. It is ever-evolving and pulling from all corners of Italy, Eastern Europe, Morocco, France and India.

It is playful, exuberant and passionate.

Chef Clark's food is artistic and creative in the best of ways. "My brain spins on ideas," he said. He collects these ideas much like he collects chile peppers (an obsession that plays out in beautifully spiced ways) and cookbooks: with enthusiasm and glee. His cookbook collection holds more than 250 volumes. And chile peppers? If you get him talking about peppers, you'll need some time. Trinadad Sunshine, Naga Jolokia and Moruga Scorpion—he's an open encyclopedia when it comes to chiles and you'll often see them used at Wildwood in the most discerning and exciting ways, like in the Fire Roasted Pork Chop where green chile harissa meets crushed potatoes, broccoli and the house-made pickled Calabrians.

The menu is always changing, based on what is fresh and available from sustainable sources. The desserts are a gorgeous and fitting ending to every memorable meal at Wildwood. Pastry Chef Julianne Richardson has created a menu that holds some of the most thoughtful, beautifully presented sweet treats in all of Portland. A Dark Chocolate Enrobed Pumpkin Panna Cotta laced with truffle popcorn

The Right Ingredients

Duck fat can be purchased at most grocery stores and butcher shops. If you don't have access to a smoker for the Smoked Potatoes, smoked salt will work great, too.

brittle and vanilla anglaise, for example, served on a rustic piece of pottery, might just be the best little gift you can give yourself.

For a guy that grew up in the middle of South Dakota, Chef Clark has proven himself a mainstay on the Portland dining scene and his playful sense of class is a welcome ingredient of this long-revered establishment located near Forest Park's 30-mile-long Wildwood Trail. And the tomatoes? If you're curious, we bet you can find a few jars hidden under the chef's desk, but don't tell him we told you.

DUCK CONFIT
With Kimchi Stew and Smoked Potatoes

(Serves 4)

4   duck legs trimmed of excess fat
2   Tbs kosher salt
1   tsp black pepper, coarsely ground
4   bay leaves, crushed
4   cups duck fat

• Season legs with salt and spices. Let set overnight. • Rinse off seasoning leaving some residue of salt and peppercorns. • Preheat oven to 200°. • Heat duck fat in a braising pan large enough to hold duck legs and fat. • Plunge duck into warm fat and place in the oven. • Cook until duck is tender about 6-8 hours. • Cool duck in fat overnight. At this point duck can be stored in a refrigerator for one month. • Remove duck from fat. • Heat a sauté pan over medium high heat. • Add a little duck fat and sear until skin is crispy. • Flip over and reduce heat. • Cook until duck is warm through.

KIMCHI

1   lb Napa cabbage, large dice
½   large daikon radish, batonnet
2   carrots, batonnet
1   bunch scallions, batonnet
3   oz ginger peeled, sliced
1   head garlic, peeled and sliced
½   cup Korean chile powder, fine grind
½   cup fish sauce
½   cup water

• Combine garlic, ginger, chile powder, fish sauce and water in a blender.
• Toss with cabbage and vegetables.
• Pack mixture in a crock or mason jars. • Ferment to desired level. Can substitute store-bought, if necessary.

KIMCHI STEW

1   lb bacon, medium diced
1   medium onion, sliced
8   oz mushrooms, sliced
2   Tbs sesame oil
1   cup chicken stock
    Lime juice

• Heat saucepan over medium heat.
• Add sesame oil and bacon. • Saute until bacon starts to caramelize. • Add

mushrooms and onion. • Cook until tender about 5-8 minutes. • Add kimchi and broth. • Let liquid reduce until saucy. • Finish with lime juice.

SMOKED POTATOES

1   lb waxy potatoes
3   nori sheets
½   head garlic, roasted
3   Tbs sesame oil
1   tsp champagne vinegar

• Cook potatoes in highly salted water until fork tender. • Drain and chill. • Light smoker and smoke over hardwood for 4 hours. (Smoking can be omitted). • Dice potatoes and crisp up in a sauté pan.
• Combine nori, garlic, oil and vinegar.
• Toss potatoes with mixture.

RINGSIDE FISH HOUSE

FOR SOME CHEFS, THE FIRST SEEDS of restaurant life are planted as early as elementary school. "At show and tell, I was the kid that brought in the snail shells from dinner the night before," said Chef David Ezelle.

Growing up in Southern California, David was part of a big, bustling extended family. His aunt owned a restaurant called The Bay Marie, where he and his parents would frequent for dinner. He described the place as "French-y" and a bit fancy. Obviously, from the snail shells, he was up to the dining experience even as a young boy.

But it wasn't until college that David realized he wanted to be a chef. He went to school at the Culinary Institute of America in Hyde Park, New York before bopping around the country gaining noteworthy experiences that would lead him into the highest position at RingSide Fish House in Portland.

"I learned rather quickly that it's not enough to be able to cook. It's a balance between your creative side with the understanding that this is a business," said David.

RingSide's commitment to high standards and the best product available has allowed David the fortune of working simply with fantastic ingredients.

Wild and Coho salmon, as well as steelhead, represent the Northwest region and are some of David's favorite fish to prepare. Delivered fresh from the Quinault and Columbia Rivers, the fish are "indicative of the area and what we're blessed to have," said David. Local oysters, Dungeness crab, king salmon, Alaskan halibut and dayboat sea scallops can also be found.

Fresh fish of the highest quality doesn't need much, except to be cooked to perfection. This is where David excels. You won't find utterly complex dishes on his menu. You'll find simple, edited ingredients that highlight the very best seafood. In fact the menu is broken up into two seafood sections: Fish House Offerings and Simple Fish. Where the Trout Almondine shines with marcona almonds and sauce Meuniere, the Roasted Wild Halibut is just that, perfectly roasted halibut with traditional sides. Where the Seared Day Boat Scallops impress with squid ink gnocchi, sofrito, crispy ham and lemon sabayon, the Grilled Swordfish is exactly as you know it to be.

The Maine Lobster Pasta is really something special. The house-made spaghetti dances with tomato, tarragon cream and fresh Maine lobster meat and once again shows the beauty of simple flavors and the very best ingredients.

RingSide Fish House is not all seafood. A fine selection of dry-aged, all-natural Angus beef from Washington State fills out the menu with Prime Rib, Filet Mignon, New York Strip and Rib Eye.

Located on the second floor of the Fox Tower, the 250-seat restaurant overlooks Director Park in downtown Portland and is the perfect spot for business lunches, dinner dates, happy hours and special occasions.

When you watch David shuck an oyster or filet the first delivery of the season's Copper River sockeye, you can't help but think of the little boy that once showed off his snail shells.

Photos Rich Shafer

CEDAR PLANKED STEELHEAD
With Whole Grain Mustard, Rosemary & Preserved Lemon

(Serves 6 to 8)

1	4 lb steelhead or salmon filet, pin bones removed, skin on
1x8	cedar plank, 20 inches long, soaked in cold water for 1 hour
¾	cup whole grain mustard
¾	cup maple syrup
2	Tbs chopped fresh rosemary leaves
⅓	cup lemon preserves
½	cup olive oil
	Kosher salt and black pepper to taste

• Combine mustard, syrup, rosemary and lemon preserves in a bowl and mix well. • Set aside.

• Brush steelhead flesh with olive oil and season with salt and pepper.

• Place steelhead, flesh side down first, on medium high heated grill and cook for 2 minutes.

• Before turning, brush skin side of steelhead with olive oil and season with salt and pepper. • Carefully turn steelhead over onto skin side and cook another 2 minutes.

• Remove steelhead from grill and place onto cedar plank, skin side down.

• Spread mustard glaze evenly over the steelhead.

• Increase grill heat to high, place cedar plank onto grill and close the lid. • Cook for about 8 to 10 minutes or until fish just begins to flake when pulled apart with a fork.

• Serve immediately from the smoking cedar plank.

Fish Sense

Fish takes a lot less time than you think it does. It's also important to remember that fish waits for no one. Once it's done, you have to serve it immediately.

—Chef David Ezelle

RINGSIDE FISH HOUSE   838 SW PARK AVENUE · RINGSIDEFISHHOUSE.COM   503.227.3900

25

Photos Tyson Robichaud

SMALLWARES

ON AN AVERAGE MORNING IN JULY, knee-deep in restaurant office work, Smallwares chef-owner Johanna Ware noticed a tweet about a *New York Times* story on the Portland food scene.

Like many Portland restaurant owners did that morning, she clicked the link to read more.

"I had no idea we were going to be in that article," said Johanna. "I got to the bottom and thought, 'Oh. My. God.'"

The article, which featured four Portland restaurants on the "grown-up" side of the city's booming food renaissance included

Smallwares and described a first experience with Johanna's inauthentic Asian cuisine as "hard to deny the pleasures of."

That inauthentic Asian cuisine, being turned out in a 80-seat labor of love Beaumont neighborhood space, is reflective of a chef that spent the early part of her career sporting a rookie title at two impressive Manhattan addresses, Public and Momofuku. The ingredients she experimented with, particularly while at Public, were "crazy" and foreign to her at the time—things like sumac that brilliantly flavored the free-spirited fusion cuisine Public is known for.

Then, when she went on to Momofuku, her love for learning Japanese and Korean became full-fledged and informed under the brilliant direction of David Chang.

"I wouldn't be cooking the food I am without Public and Momofuku," said Johanna.

But that didn't stop her from eventually saying goodbye to the city that afforded her such opportunity. Ready to leave the New York game and set sites on a new locale, she and her husband moved to Portland, where the living was cheap, the food scene was on the cusp, and the chefs sported t-shirts instead of stuffy coats.

"I thought it was so weird that everyone was wearing t-shirts," laughed Johanna. "I couldn't figure out how they don't burn themselves wearing short sleeves all the time. But now, I've embraced it. It's nice to wear a t-shirt every day."

Once the culture shock of t-shirt-clad kitchen masters wore off, Johanna discovered a freedom of expression and an open avenue to explore her addiction to and knowledge of quirky,

Salt the hell out of your food. People don't realize how much seasoning restaurants use. I use Diamond kosher salt. That's all I use.

—Chef Johanna Ware

tongue-numbing spices and Asian cuisine. Smallwares opened in February 2012 on the concept of small, shareable plates and creative house cocktails.

You'll find hot and spicy soups and stews (did we mention that Johanna loves spice?), three types of house-made kimchi (cabbage, daikon or apple), and inventive takes on dishes like Scallop Sashimi served with den miso, shallot and puffed rice, and Oxtail Curry with scotch bonnet, plantain chips and coconut.

The red-lacquered tables, open kitchen, glowing lanterns and blazing fireplace finish the picture of a hip yet cozy, inventive yet familiar, and quite simply awesome place to dine with friends.

Reading Johanna's menu is like reading the story of her life, which really is the very best kind of food experience.

FRIED KALE WITH FISH SAUCE AND BACON

(Serves 4)

1   bunch of kale (Johanna prefers Cavolo Nero, but any will do)
8   cups canola oil
    Tempura Batter (recipe follows)
½   cup Fish Sauce Dressing (recipe follows)
¼   cup chopped, cooked thick cut bacon (the smokier the better)
2   Tbs chopped cilantro
2   Tbs chopped mint

• Bring a pot of salted water to boil.
• Tear kale leaves off of the stems, and cut larger leaves in half. • Boil kale in salted water for 1 min. • Strain into colander and spread out onto a sheet tray. • When cool enough to handle squeeze out all of the water from the kale.

• Heat 8 cups of canola oil in a wide high sided pot to 350°. • In a large bowl put fish sauce dressing, cilantro, mint, and candied bacon. • Dip the kale into the tempura and place into the oil. It is important to try and separate the leaves as it goes in the oil to avoid clumping.
• Fry for 30 sec. • Using a spider,

take kale out of oil and place into the large bowl. • Toss the kale so all the ingredients coat it. • Place into individual bowls.

TEMPURA BATTER

2   cups rice flour
1   egg
1   cup cold seltzer water
    Dash of salt

• Whisk all ingredients until they just come together.

FISH SAUCE DRESSING

½   cup fish sauce
¼   cup water
2   Tbs rice wine vinegar
6   Tbs sugar
1   lime, juiced
1   garlic clove minced
1   serrano chile minced, (keep seeds if you like it spicy)

• Whisk all ingredients together. Store in fridge, keeps for a couple weeks.

SERRATTO

SERRATTO IS THE LIVELY AND elegant neighborhood restaurant you'll find on the corner of NW 21st and Kearney. Serving authentic and innovative dishes from Italy, France and the greater Mediterranean region, the seasonal menu focuses on natural meats, the freshest seafood, and locally grown fruits and vegetables.

The longevity and history of the space, which houses old beams and woods that have been on this corner for as long as anyone can remember, adds a touch of romance and warmth that owner Julie Bond says makes Serratto a place you want to come home to.

On any given Tuesday, you'll find a table having a business meeting next to a family enjoying dinner after soccer practice. In the summer, the elegant, patio-style tables line the sidewalk outside and remind passers-by of a Tuscan village.

Chef Tony Meyers' menu is filled with hand-selected local, organic produce, meats and seafood that are all used in beautiful presentations of Northwest-inspired Mediterranean dishes. Born of a Sicilian grandmother, Italian cuisine has always been close to his heart. His house-made pastas include rigatoni, pappardelle, spaghetti, cavatelli and ravioli. They are incorporated with rich sauces such as a pork and beef Bolognese, or on the lighter side, black tiger shrimp with smoked onion, preserved lemons, watercress and dill crème.

The Anderson Ranches Lamb Osso Bucco shows off the beauty of a true braise, the perfect companion to a cold winter night. Served with herb spaetzle, forest mushrooms, cabbage and pecan gremolata, this dish beckons a slow evening with family, great wine, and a friendly, neighborhood atmosphere where candles flicker gently and laughter is all around.

The relationships Chef Meyers builds with local purveyors are of utmost importance at Serratto. Magical heirloom tomatoes, sweet basil, and Italian heirloom sweet peppers arrive in the summer handpicked and hand-delivered by a local farmer. Sweet beyond belief carrots arrive by way of Joseph, Oregon. Local chanterelles and huckleberries take tasteful forms when in-season. Meat and game are sourced from Tails & Trotters, Painted Hills Natural Beef and Anderson Ranch.

> ## Flour Power
>
> *When making pasta, be sure to keep sheets heavily floured with semolina as you work it through the pasta machine.*
>
> —Chef Tony Meyers

Be sure to say hello to bartender Kurt, who has been behind their bar for the last 30+ years. With a full bar and outstanding wine list, you will surely discover the perfect pairing for your Serratto dinner, lunch or happy hour.

With a beautiful dining room appropriate for discerning adults and children alike, a relaxed lounge, and friendly and knowledgeable service, you will always find the perfect table at Serratto.

SPAGHETTI BOLOGNESE
With Grana Padano Crisp

(Serves 8)

THE BOLOGNESE

Plan on allowing the sauce to simmer for up to 4 hours.

2	lbs ground pork
1	lb ground beef
1	cup finely diced carrot (peeled)
1	cup finely diced yellow onion
1	cup finely diced celery
1	Tbs chopped garlic
1	tsp salt
1	tsp pepper
1½	cups white wine
1	28 oz can whole peeled tomatoes
1	14 oz can whole peeled tomatoes
3	cups chicken stock
1	bay leaf
2	Tbs chopped fresh thyme
1¼	cup heavy cream
	Salt and pepper to taste

• Season the pork and beef with salt and pepper. • Brown the meat together in a large stockpot on medium high heat.

• Add the diced carrot, onion, celery, garlic, salt and pepper and cook until tender (about ten minutes). • Add the white wine and tomatoes and cook until liquid is reduced by about half. • Lower heat to a simmer, add the chicken stock and bay leaf and let simmer until sauce is reduced to a ragu-like consistency, for up to 4 hours.

• Take off the heat and stir in the thyme, cream and salt and pepper to taste.

HOMEMADE PASTA

To make pasta you need a pasta machine. There are many different kinds; a simple hand crank works great. Any noodle will go well with the meat sauce.

1¾	cups all purpose flour
6	egg yolks
1	whole egg
1½	tsp extra virgin olive oil
2	tsp water

• On a clean table create a well out of the flour, pour yolks, egg, water and olive oil in the center of the well. • Using your fingers, slowly stir the mixture counter clockwise breaking and blending the yolks together. • Slowly add in the flour at the top of the well little by little. • Once all the flour is incorporated and a dough is formed, knead the dough with both hands until smooth. • Now you are ready to make your noodle of choice with your pasta maker.

• Cook pasta in salted water for about 2 minutes, test for doneness before draining pasta.

GRANA PADANO CRISP

Grana Padano is an Italian cheese similar to Parmesan.

• To make the crisp garnish for the Bolognese bake finely minced Grana at 350° until lightly browned (check in 5 minutes). • Drape over a spoon to form desired shape until hardened.

THE PARISH

THERE IS A RESTAURANT in the Pearl District where oysters, champagne, and Southern-inspired New American cuisine rule the roost.

The Parish, the slightly upscale sister to EaT: An Oyster Bar (see page 46), answers the calling for French Quarter cuisine and ambiance, in the heart of a city that couldn't be further away geographically from the epicenter of Gumbo- and Étouffée-inspired living.

Following their success at EaT on the northside, owners Tobias Hogan and Ethan Powell decided to bring their Cajun and Creole goodness to a second, more formal location. The Parish is full of uptown flavor, both in food and atmosphere that is purposely reminiscent of upscale New Orleans.

"While EaT is a place you'll find just outside of the French Quarter in New Orleans, The Parish is the place you'll find in Uptown New Orleans or the Garden District.

More polished, more refined, but still full of traditional flavors," said Tobias.

The menu includes dishes such as Grilled Louisiana Shrimp with pimento chili sauce, Southern Fried Chicken with a house-made biscuit, brown gravy and zucchini squash slaw, and Braised Beef Short Ribs with Merchand de Vin sauce, radish gratin and wild miner's lettuce. This is polished, stylish food, using the very best ingredients and local sources whenever possible.

You'll also find farm-fresh Northwest oysters at their peak, Ethan and Tobias' calling card and sincere passion.

Prior to opening EaT, and upon moving west, Ethan began thinking about the gorgeous oyster farms lining the west coast, from northern California to Canada. Despite the grand availability of the seemingly luxurious bivalve, there weren't many places to eat and buy Northwest oysters in Portland at an affordable price.

In an effort to help create an oyster-eating culture in Portland, Ethan and Tobias needed to bring wholesale, farm-direct oysters that could be served within hours of harvest. It was a great idea that now puts the two restaurants at the top of the oyster food chain, serving a whopping 800-1,000 dozen each week, and has inspired Ethan to educate Portlanders about the benefits of oyster farming.

> *You can't get more local and organic than a Northwest oyster. They are the most sustainable food source on the planet.*
>
> —Ethan Powell,
> chef and co-owner

"You can't get more local and organic than a Northwest oyster," said Ethan. "They are the most sustainable food source on the planet."

For those interested in learning more about oysters and oyster farming in the Northwest, be on the lookout for the Oyster Bus, an educational tour where riders learn from Ethan about the variety of oysters available along the coast including Tillamook, Penn Cove and Hama Hama varieties.

The bus's destination is an oyster farm where riders enjoy tastings, of oysters of course, along with a grilled lunch, wine and beer pairings.

The Parish also serves a noteworthy and colorful Sunday brunch where Homemade Sticky Buns dance with a Dungeness Crab Cake and live original New Orleans jazz.

This is what the Old New Orleans looks like in Portland. So go ahead, pull up a chair and order yourself a glass of Argyle Sparkling Brut and a dozen Hama Hamas while you decide what you'd like for dinner. You deserve it.

Bloom It

It's important to 'bloom' saffron before you use it. Let it sit in room temperature water for ten minutes before adding to your recipe. You'll be amazed by the increased intensity of flavor.

—Ethan Powell, chef and co-owner

CRAWFISH RAVIOLI IN SAFFRON CREAM SAUCE

(Serves 7)

If you can't find crawfish tails, you can easily substitute shrimp, dungeness crab or lump crabmeat.

CRAWFISH STUFFING

Extra virgin olive oil
1   Tbs garlic, chopped
2   cups yellow onion, chopped
1   cup celery, chopped
1   cup green bell pepper, chopped
1   Tbs kosher salt
1   tsp black pepper, fresh ground
½   lb crawfish tails, rough chopped
Juice and zest of one lemon
Juice and zest of one lime
Juice and zest of one orange
3   whole eggs
1   cup breadcrumbs

• In sauté pan heat oil over medium-high heat. • When hot add garlic, sauté for a minute. • Add onion, sauté a minute add celery and pepper. • Cook until softened, add salt and pepper, let cool.

• Beat eggs and add all other ingredients. • Store in fridge. This can be made a day in advance.

RAVIOLI PASTA

14   oz flour
5   whole eggs, beaten well

• On a work surface make a well with the flour, add eggs and slowly mix to form dough. • Add more flour if really sticky. • Form into a circle and let rest at room temp for 30 minutes. • Using a pasta roller start at level 7 and feed the pasta through the roller until you get to level 2. • Using a cookie cutter, cut circles through the pasta.

• To form the ravioli, brush circles with egg wash, add 1 tablespoon of crawfish mix. • Top with ravioli circle and crimp edges to form a seal. These can be made a day before and stored covered in a refrigerator.

SAFFRON SAUCE

1   Tbs garlic, chopped
1   Tbs extra virgin olive oil
2   cups cream
⅛   oz saffron, bloomed

• In a small saucepan, sauté garlic in oil until softened, don't let it color. Add cream and saffron. • Reduce liquid by 1/3 over low heat. • Then strain to remove bits of garlic and saffron.

• To serve ravioli, bring salted water to a boil. In another pan, heat saffron sauce over medium heat until it just simmers. • Drop ravioli into boiling water and cook until al dente (about 1 minute). • Transfer to warm sauce and cook for 30 seconds more. • Divide pasta onto plates and pour sauce over. • Add fresh grated cheese like Pecorino or Parmesan.

BESAW'S

CHEF MICHAEL UHNAK'S MORNING routine is as rooted as Besaw's itself. Upon arrival, he grabs a cup of coffee, heads out to the restaurant's backyard garden, and spends the first two hours of his day tending to the 18 raised beds he's harvested for the past four years.

"Oh man, it's so nice. Even if it's raining, I couldn't be happier to start the day out there. It keeps me grounded and earthy," says Chef Uhnak, or "Cheffy" as he's more commonly referred.

While the garden supplies Cheffy with just a fraction of the produce needed to feed the tremendous volume this popular Portland establishment sees every day, it is no less reflective of the restaurant's authentic conviction to source local.

Kale, brussels sprouts, herbs, pumpkins—the autumn garden often bestows the best ingredients for making dishes like Pumpkin Fritters served with crème fraîche and a Kale Caesar with fried anchovies, croutons and asiago. It's the kind of food that lingers with comfort and care and seasonality. The garden, and its powerful effects on the space, neighborhood

Going to Besaw's is just like going to Grandma's house.

—"Cheffy" or Chef Michael Uhnak

Photos: Lincoln Barbour

and restaurant crew, is a big part of the reason why you can't walk into Besaw's without feeling warm and well-loved.

"It's just like going to Grandma's house," said Cheffy.

That it is. A popular meeting place since 1903, Besaw's now serves breakfast, brunch, lunch and dinner in an atmosphere that reflects its history of providing neighborhood folks with a stiff drink, a scrumptious meal

and lively conversation. Besaw's genuine warmth of heart can be seen in nooks and crannies all over the restaurant, as well as in the eyes of everyone who works here. From the old, well-worn mahogany bar to the kind and familiar faces you see tableside, there is a genuine energy that brings you back to a time and place you've never been, but somehow recognize.

While the menus change weekly, there are certain dishes that claim permanent menu space, and for good reason. The Croque Madame at breakfast and brunch, made with buttered Pullman brioche, shaved ham, gruyere cheese sauce, two over-medium eggs, chives and rosemary garlic potatoes gives center stage to local cage-free eggs and 100% hormone-free dairy products. At dinner, it's a good idea to try Besaw's Legendary Meatloaf, topped with bacon and pan gravy and served with red potatoes, carrots and caramelized onions. New to the menu this winter is Cheffy's Goat Stew. Willamette Valley braised goat is simmered for three to five hours in a rich tomato sauce, a preparation that Cheffy says makes goat approachable and so incredibly easy to love.

There is also the Fried Chicken made with Draper Valley chicken breast and your choice of a cheddar-chive waffle or mashed potato, pan gravy and wilted greens. The Baked Mac is made with local cheeses from Tillamook and the Portland Creamery. The Besaw's Board is filled with local cured meats, cheeses, fresh local fruit, apricot chutney, local wild honey, house-made crackers and bread.

Notice a theme here? Local. Wild. House-made.

"If I can make it in house I will," said Cheffy.

For a chef that started out as a dishwasher in Upstate New York at the age of 15, a kid that played in his uncle's butcher shop and his grandfather's garden, you could say that Cheffy is right where he's supposed to be. He's right where the rest of us should be. At Besaw's. At home.

BESAW'S LEGENDARY MEATLOAF

(Makes 1 loaf or 10-10 oz portions)

5	lbs ground beef (90/10 fat)
½	cup mushrooms (crimini or your favorite mushroom)
1	medium yellow onion
1	Tbs chopped garlic
½	cup oats
½	cup panko crumbs
2	eggs
1½	Tbs balsamic
4-6	slices bacon
2	tsp salt
1	tsp pepper

• Pulse the mushrooms, onions and garlic in a food processor. • Drop the puréed mix into a sauté pan with the balsamic vinegar, reduce on medium heat till most of the liquid is gone.

• Combine the sautéed mixture with the ground beef, eggs, salt and pepper, oats and panko crumbs. • Mix thoroughly.

• Form into a loaf and cover the top of your meatloaf with the strips of bacon.

• Place on an oiled baking sheet to go into the oven.

• Preheat the oven to 225°. • Bake meatloaf for about 45 minutes or until the center of the meatloaf reaches 155°.

• Remove meatloaf from the oven and let rest before slicing. This will make your slices picture perfect.

BOLLYWOOD THEATER

JUST HOURS AFTER signing the lease on his soon-to-be Indian restaurant on Alberta, chef-owner Troy MacLarty hopped on a plane to India, for the very first time.

Nick Holmboe

Bollywood Theater was an idea born out of the free-flowing, authentic Indian food outposts of Berkeley, California, where Troy trained under fine-dining legends at Chez Panisse. He ate Indian food with a passion. He craved it.

After moving to Portland and realizing that good Indian street food could not be found, he began to teach himself how to recreate the flavors and preparations he loved so much in Berkeley. He spent a solid year and a half learning the cuisine, the techniques, the flavors, the spices. He hosted friends for Indian-inspired dinner parties every Friday night. He read every Indian food publication he could get his hands on.

"I own every good Indian cookbook made in the last fifteen years. I was cooking the food I loved to eat," said Troy.

But he had never been to India.

Jeremy Fenske

Although it was a coincidence that he signed that lease on the exact day he hopped on a plane for his first trek to India, you could say that the chance circumstance was indicative of the thoughtful spirit that backs this *Oregonian*-named Rising Star of 2013.

"That first trip was less about food and more about culture. My inclination was that we weren't going to see in India what we have in the U.S.," said Troy.

He traveled with purpose, to areas underrepresented in restaurants here in the states—to Mumbai and the southern part of the country where seasonality veers to the lighter end of traditional street cuisine. He tasted, on some epic days, upwards of 20 dishes in a short window of time, but of greater importance to him, he observed the feelings, the people, the connections, the energy.

What he found was movement, chaos, transportation, and color. He found people that were accepting and welcoming. He wasn't collecting recipes. He already had those back at home in Portland. He was collecting sights and sounds and smells, along with the affirmation that what he had spent so much time learning was authentic and spot-on. He returned to Portland with ideas, inspiration, trinkets and postcards, steel cups and plates, and the desire to capture that movement and energy and color in the small, warehouse-like, garage door-lined space that was waiting for him on NE Alberta Street.

Troy's inspiration translated quite well. Bollywood Theater is now serving upwards of 1500 plates a day. This is classic Indian street food served on steel plates and cups, just like you'd find in Mumbai, food that is winning the approval of westerners and Indian-Americans and pretty much anyone that walks up to the counter and orders Papri Chaat or Kati Roll or Vada Pav with an ice cold Thum's Up.

"It's never been my goal to reinvent," said Troy.

And therein lies the magic. Samosa Cholle are popular with westerners because they are familiar and approachable, filled with spiced potatoes, onions, ginger and peas and topped with chickpea chole and green chutney. Vada Pav that is adored by Indian-Americans because it is just what they remember feasting on as children—a spicy potato dumpling dipped in chickpea batter and fried, then served on a roll with chutneys. It is the "poor man's burger" of Mumbai and a memory-driven treat for many in Portland's Indian community.

For Troy, it is the Papri Chaat that sums up what

Home cooks get shackled with the idea of a recipe. Look outside the box. There is no definite magic written in the words. Make mistakes, go back and do it again, make changes. Try again.

—Chef Troy MacLarty

Bollywood Theater is all about. House-made crackers topped with chickpeas, potatoes, yogurt, cilantro and tamarind chutney, this dish is bright and immediate—in perfect balance with that lighter end of the Indian food spectrum he was searching for in Mumbai.

"I want people to have that experience, as if they have gone some place," said Troy.

And soon they will be able to travel even more, as Troy gets ready to open his second Bollywood Theater location on 30th and Division. Look for a bigger restaurant space coupled with an Indian grocery where his team will be able to enjoy the freedom that comes from 4,000 feet of space and guests will be able to purchase select Indian spices and ingredients.

ROASTED BEETS
With Coconut Milk, Curry Leaves and Indian Spices

12 medium red beets, roasted, peeled and cut into 1" pieces

4 medium gold beets, roasted, peeled and cut into 1" pieces

2 Tbs white wine vinegar

Salt, to taste

Coconut milk marinade (recipe follows)

Beet Seeds (recipe follows)

½ bunch cilantro, roughly chopped

• Toss roasted beets (separately) with white wine vinegar and salt. • Allow to macerate for 30 minutes, then toss with coconut milk marinade. • Place red beets on plate, topped with gold beets. • Drizzle Beet Seeds over beets and top with chopped cilantro.

Troy Maclartn

BEET SEEDS

1 tsp cumin seeds

1 tsp nigella seeds

1 tsp yellow mustard seeds

1 tsp black mustard seeds

¼ cup canola oil

• Toast all spices in oil over low to medium heat until lightly browned. Cumin is the best indicator of doneness.

• Allow to cool to room temperature.

COCONUT MILK MARINADE

15 curry leaves

1 serrano chile, thinly sliced

1 shallot, thinly sliced

2 Tbs canola oil

1 can coconut milk

¼ cup white wine vinegar

Salt, as needed

• Saute curry leaves, shallots and serrano chiles with canola oil over medium heat, until curry leaves are toasted and crispy.

• Add coconut milk, bring to a simmer and cook until reduced by one fourth.

• Add white wine vinegar and adjust seasoning with salt. • Allow to cool to room temperature.

DAVIS STREET TAVERN

IN 1996, CHRISTOPHER Handford opened his first bottle of champagne as a server in Nantucket with an audience that included Tracy Root, the veteran island restaurateur. It was a memorable moment for a young man that would move on to work in some of the country's top restaurants.

"I did it totally wrong," laughed Christopher, now owner of Portland's Davis Street Tavern and Jamison.

If you know anything about Christopher Handford, this is an endearing look at the very beginning of a career that has since earned him impressive accomplishments in American fine dining which include working for Tom Colicchio's Craft and Todd English's Olives, experiences Christopher refers to as his "PhD." His resume also includes several luxurious restaurants on the famously elite and white tablecloth-clad island of Nantucket, where his love affair with fine dining really began, back with that first bottle of champagne.

But when the well-versed Handford moved to Portland eight years ago, he was searching for a way out of the machine that is the Northeast. He was looking for an

Thomas Boyd

experience that was more laid back, but still elegant. The environs of the Northwest, and specifically, an early 20th century building in the middle of Old Town Portland beckoned a new idea.

Handford opened Davis Street Tavern with his cousin Blake Smith five years ago at the bottom of the recession, with the goal of reinventing the American tavern with the glisten of fine

dining. He believed that comfort food could be upscale, and that American classics like macaroni and cheese and New York strip steak and burgers and fish tacos could be done really well. He believed that handsome, history-rich recessed wood and iron-cast chandeliers weren't reserved for bar clientele, but rather could give a top-notch dining experience the rough notes of elegance a white tablecloth never could.

"Our thought was, this idea, this upscale American tavern, was the best thing for this neighborhood," said Handford. And he was right.

With the addition of Executive Chef Gavin Ledson, the Davis Street Tavern is now one of the best places in the city to have a business lunch. It's also home to a macaroni and cheese that is so delicious, it's sought-after with fervor. The Velvety Mac 'n Cheese, which is essentially a 3-cheese béchamel with pasta, started as a side dish to the roast chicken.

"They wanted it at happy hour, they wanted it at lunch, they wanted it at dinner, they wanted it all the time," said Handford.

The mac 'n cheese typifies the Davis Street Tavern experience, one that elevates without excluding. The Dungeness Crab Bisque includes notes of sautéed fennel and

Pernod. The Anderson Ranch Lamb Burger excites with Mediterranean flavors of feta, apricot and mint. The Carlton Farms Center Cut Pork Chop is served with a warm bacon-pear vinaigrette, escarole and white bean puree. This is comfort food brushed with an elegance that makes each visit to Davis Street Tavern familiar and yet incredibly special.

Christopher Handford perfected his table-side champagne presentation long ago, of course. And in case you're curious, you will find champagne flutes among the comfort food and wood and brick at Davis Street. You will not, however, find white tablecloths.

Jamison in the Pearl District is also owned by Christopher Handford. See page 44 to learn more about his second restaurant.

DUNGENESS CRAB BISQUE

Live crabs will make the bisque taste the best versus the typical cooked and frozen crabs at most seafood counters.

- 2 Dungeness crabs, split
- ¼ lb carrots, chopped
- ¼ lb onion, chopped
- ¼ lb celery, chopped
- ¼ lb fennel, chopped
- 2 cloves garlic, lightly crushed
  Olive oil
- 32 oz water
- 32 oz clam juice
- 2 Tbs tomato paste
- 2 cups heavy cream
- 2 Tbs lemon juice
- 1 sprig tarragon
- ¼ lb butter
- ¼ oz flour
- 1 oz Pernod
  Salt and pepper to taste
  Lemon
  Fresh fine herbs, parsley, chives, tarragon and chervil, finely chopped
  Butter

• Spread chopped carrots, onion, celery, fennel and garlic (your mirepoix) on a sheet pan, drizzle with olive oil, and place split crab on top. • Pull off half the legs to use later for garnish. • Roast at 400º until golden. • Remove from oven and place all into a large stockpot. • Add tomato paste, clam juice and water. • Allow to simmer to meld the flavors, for about 20-30 minutes. • Strain broth into another pot and whisk in the cream to the broth. • Discard the vegetables and crab. • Add the tarragon sprig and let steep for 5 minutes off heat. • Season with salt and pepper. • Remove tarragon sprig, add Pernod and test for seasoning.

• Make a simple roux with the butter and flour in order to adjust consistency. • Heat butter in a pan over medium heat, add flour all at once while whisking vigorously. • When the butter and flour begins to thin and bubble, reduce heat to low. • Cook and whisk occasionally until you smell a toasty aroma, then cook a few minutes more stirring occasionally. The roux can be used immediately to thicken the bisque at room temperature, or let the roux cool down first before adding if the bisque is hot.

• Bisque can be kept hot for up to an hour before being served. • For service take legs that were pulled before rest of the Dungeness crab was roasted, blanch with lemon and salt. • Let cool. • Break legs to remove crab meat, then sauté with butter and fine herbs. • Pour bisque into bowls and top with sautéed crab as garnish.

CAFÉ NELL

IN THE HEART OF NORTHWEST

Portland, there is a little gem of a neighborhood restaurant where French-inspired American classics are prepared simply from Northwest ingredients.

But even more than the food, if at all possible because the food is outstanding in the most comforting of ways, owner Vanessa Preston says it is the love that exists within every corner of this space that has allowed Café Nell to bloom into the neighborhood destination it is today.

"Portland has all of these amazing restaurants, but where is the go-to restaurant? Where is there a place where you can go every day and be welcomed and celebrated?" asked Vanessa.

This idea, that a neighborhood restaurant can live up to savvy diners' expectations and still offer a welcoming atmosphere that begs visits time and time again, is what has come to fruition at Café Nell, now in its fifth year of operation.

Vibrant. Energized. Classic. Full of color and warmth that hosts a crowd of regulars so connected and neighborly that several feel, and act said Vanessa rather lovingly, like they own the place.

The interior sparkles like a little jewelry box and lights up the corner of 20th and Kearney. In the winter months, candles flicker and a giant fireplace blazes with light that seems to hit every piece of glass and angle in the most glorious way. Even Vanessa sparkles, with a social savoir-faire that is intoxicating, real and adored by everyone who meets her.

"Now when I'm at a dinner party, practically everyone else in attendance is someone I met at Café Nell," said Vanessa.

The same holds true for the servers and kitchen staff as well as the regulars of Café Nell who build friendships and even support each other through the toughest of times.

Chef Ethan Flom points to dishes such as the Lamb Ragu, Steak Frites and Wild Mushroom Risotto. The hearty, warm and comforting flavors are reflective of both his personal style and the

Cook with love, passion and energy. Never give up.
—Chef Ethan Flom

feeling that Café Nell puts out into the world. An alum of Broder in SE Portland, Chef Ethan said he made his way on his own through the culinary scene. He started cooking when "cooking" meant experimenting with eggs on his little sister's Easy Bake Oven. He never gave up that inquisitive nature and eventually found himself cooking for dinner parties while attending the University of Oregon in Eugene.

"It's always been more of a love thing than a school thing," said Chef Ethan.

You can taste that love in everything Chef Ethan puts out at Café Nell. Whether it is a classic Salmon Tartare or Steak Wellington, the Chicken Paillard or Baked Mac & Cheese with blue, Gruyere and Tillamook cheddar cheeses, there is an elevated skill and quintessential flavor that fits this restaurant, this space, this namesake of Vanessa's mother Nell, so very, very well.

So pull up a chair next to the crackling fire and set your sights on Café Nell's Butter Poached Oregon Rockfish or Oven Roasted Chicken. Take your time with a classic Maker's Mark Manhattan and a warm bowl of Lamb Ragu served over pappardelle noodles. It's going to be a long winter. You need some new friends, a cozy destination, and food that impresses not with waiting lists and counter service and inventive preparations, but with simple, great flavors dusted with candlelight.

Oh, and don't forget Bottomless Bubbles every Saturday night 6pm-close where you can feast on champagne to your heart's desire. Thursday is Date Night: Two people, one starter, two entrees, one bottle of wine, all for $45. And there's always Oregon's #1 Bloody Mary, the Mary Nell, served at Sunday Brunch. Yes, all of that sounds rather friendly and celebratory, too. We'll see you at the Nell.

CAFÉ NELL LAMB RAGU

- 1 carrot (preferably organic), finely diced
- 1 red onion (preferably organic), finely diced
- 1 celery rib, finely diced
- 1½ lbs braised lamb shank meat, pulled off the bone
- 2 tsp ground coriander
- 1 tsp ground fennel seeds
- ½ tsp ground cumin
- 1 tsp chopped fresh rosemary
- 1 tsp chopped fresh thyme
   Kosher salt and freshly ground pepper (to taste)
- 1 Tbsp tomato paste
- ½ cup dry red wine
- 1 28-oz can diced tomatoes
- 1¼ cups chicken stock or low-sodium broth
- ¾ lb dried pappardelle noodles
- 1 Tbs unsalted butter
- 1 cup heavy cream
- 1 Tbs minced garlic
- 1 Tbs minced shallots
- ½ cup shredded Parmesan cheese

• In a large enamel coated cast-iron casserole, heat 2 tablespoons of the oil. • Add the carrot, onion and celery and cook over high heat, stirring occasionally, until slightly softened, about five minutes. • Add the pre-braised lamb, coriander, fennel, cumin, rosemary and thyme. • Season with salt and pepper. • Cook, stirring until the liquid evaporates, about five minutes.

• Stir in the tomato paste. • Add wine and cook until just evaporated, about five minutes. • Add tomatoes and their juices, along with chicken stock and bring to a boil, then quickly reduce to a simmer. • Cover partially; simmer over moderately low heat until the liquid is slightly reduced, 25 to 30 minutes.

• In a large pot of boiling salted water, cook pasta until just al dente, being careful not to overcook pasta, since it will be sautéed with sauce. • Drain, shaking well.

• Melt butter in a hot 12" sauté pan. • Add garlic and shallots, being careful not to burn the butter shallot mixture. • Add cream and reduce by half. Add cooked pasta and cheese.

• Sauté pasta with sauce just until sauce is melted and creamy, being careful not to destroy the noodles or overcook them. • Mound portion into generous bowl with kitchen tongs. • Ladle lamb ragu atop. • Garnish with grated Parmesan cheese.

BRASSERIE MONTMARTRE

🍴 CHEF JOHNNY NUNN GREW up in a foodie household where Galloping Gourmet, Julia Childs, dinner parties, and his mother's Oysters Baltimore ruled the roost.

But, at the age of 26, when he decided to leave his job with Charles Schwab in San Francisco to pursue a restaurant career, his gourmand family wasn't as enthused as one might anticipate. "Fifteen years ago, it wasn't quite as romantic as it is now, especially for male chefs," said Johnny.

Of no matter at the time to Johnny however, he leapt full-force into his first gig as the runner boy at Aqua and never looked back. Step by step he moved farther and farther away from San Francisco's financial district.

"It was a quick study. A total immersion thing. I was cooking sixteen hours a day. I went after it tirelessly," he said.

Chef Johnny's bootcamp mentality has served him well. His resume includes the James Beard award-winning kitchens of Mitchell Rosenthal of Town Hall Restaurant in San Francisco and Irving Street Kitchen in Portland, and of Daniel Humm of Eleven Madison Park in New York. Most recently, and prior to joining Brasserie Montmartre, he was executive chef at Ringside Fish House in Portland.

Peter Brock

Moving from Ringside to the Brasserie was one of the easier ventures of his career, geographically speaking, as the two restaurants are located on the same block.

"Conveniently, I still have the same parking spot," laughed Johnny.

He is now cooking French-American, approachable, brasserie food. It is food to drink by, in a location where history, libations and live jazz are a longstanding tradition. Where the roots of the iconic Calmut Building date back to 1907. Where Northwest ingredients mix with European treatments. Where the beer flows as freely as the red wine. Where rustic meets refined. Where giant chandeliers hang from wood-beamed walls.

Juliana Patrick

Where Paris meets Portland.

You will find a menu that teases French, but is not French in the most classic sense. Were you a true Francophile, you'd probably take one look at the menu and say that it's not French at all.

And Chef Johnny says that's perfectly fine because Brasserie Montmartre is quite careful about not labeling themselves solely for French food. They serve Crispy Frog Legs, but not escargot. Classic and delicious Steak Frites, but also a Paella that sings of Chef Johnny's time in Spain. Grilled Asparagus Salad with duck confit, arugula, and a fried duck egg. Meatballs with crimini mushrooms and *sauce au poivre*. And don't forget about the aforementioned frites—you can order them on their own as a starter, topped with garlic aioli, black truffle or duck fat.

The beers on tap rival any brewery in Portland, and in fact, the Brasserie is toying with putting a brewery downstairs. But you of course will also find great valued Oregon Pinot Noirs and big white wines, along with an inventive craft cocktail menu and one of the best happy hours in town.

All of this French-y goodness is tucked away on a tiny street in downtown Portland—a street that you don't want to pass by. It will lead you straight to a little slice of Paris in the middle of Stumptown. Find yourself a patio table with a wicker chair and red umbrella, or a seat at the bar inside where notes of live music filter through five days a week.

And be sure to look for "La Cave," a room whose walls

are filled with crayon art from coloring contests from the 1980s. The Brasserie picked up the contest last year and began adding to this popular piece of history once again.

This French-influenced American respite for food, drink and fun clearly has the markings of a chef that understands what the word brasserie means in Paris and Portland.

STEAK FRITES
With Watercress, Roasted Garlic Butter and Red Wine Gastrique

Typically Steak Frites cuts are top Sirloin, Shoulder Tenderloin, Flat Iron or Hanger. First, be sure to trim most of the fat and all of the silver skin from your cuts. The steaks can be grilled or pan seared and then roasted in the oven, whichever you prefer.

4   quality steaks, about 8 oz ea

• Season the steaks with kosher salt and pepper. Set aside while you prepare the other components of the dish.

ROASTED GARLIC BUTTER

This can be prepared several days in advance and softened before service.

1   head of fresh garlic
     Extra virgin olive oil
     Kosher salt and pepper
1   lb unsalted butter, room temperature
1   Tbs chopped thyme
1   Tbs minced shallot

• Preheat the oven to 350°. • Cut the top off of the garlic head to expose the cloves while leaving majority of the head intact. • Sprinkle with olive oil and salt and pepper. • Wrap in aluminum foil and put in the oven for about 15 minutes or until the garlic is soft to the touch and smells roasted.

• Place the butter, shallots and thyme in a large bowl. • Allow the foil/garlic to cool and carefully open. • Squeeze the roasted garlic flesh into the butter mixture and add any oil that's collected at the bottom. • Mix thoroughly with a plastic spatula and season to taste with kosher salt and pepper and reserve for plating.

Mesa Lange-Scoval

GASTRIQUE

½   cup granulated sugar
2   cups red wine (any table wine)
2   Tbs water

• In a medium sized non-reactive saucepot, add the sugar and water. • Mix thoroughly and place over a medium flame until the sugar caramelizes. • Remove from the flame and add the wine. • Reduce until it has the consistency of maple syrup.

• Serve warm.

FRITES

2   qts canola oil
2   large russet potatoes, cleaned and dried
     Kosher salt
1   bunch watercress

• Preheat a fryer or a pot of canola oil to 275°. • Using a mandolin slicer or a chef knife, julienne the potatoes and place them in a large bowl of cold water.

• Put them in the sink and allow cold water to flow over the potatoes to rinse off the starch—about 15 minutes.

• Strain the water off of the potatoes and allow them to dry thoroughly.

• Drop the russets in the oil and allow them to blanch for 6 minutes, remove from the oil, strain and refrigerate until service.

TO PLATE:

• Preheat fryer oil to 350°. • Prepare the steaks by the desired method and allow them to rest. • Drop the frites into the oil (for a second time) and cook for about 3 minutes or until crispy. • Remove from the oil with a strainer, allow the oil to drain, transfer to a large bowl and season with kosher salt and toss.

• Place the steaks on large plates. • Add frites next to steak. • Place a tablespoon of butter on top of the meat, drizzle with the gastrique and garnish with watercress.

LAURELHURST MARKET

IT'S BEEN SAID BEFORE, BUT WE'RE here to say it again. Laurelhurst Market is the steakhouse for the rest of us.

Here, the traditional notes of an American steakhouse were never part of the plan. You will not find a coat check and valet or a dark dining room lined in oak and leather. You will not be intimidated by extravagant cuts of meat that define the boys' club valedictorian lifestyle.

Laurelhurst Market is the antithesis of the steakhouse we've come to expect in America. It is a light and bright space that houses approachable price points, local-driven meats and produce, and a brotherhood of butcher boys that have successfully redefined what this concept can look like. Rustic yet elegant. Safe yet adventurous. Classic yet nuanced.

Part restaurant, part butcher shop, Laurelhurst Market is a uniquely Portland experience where you can have a Cold Smoked Rib Eye with sweet onion rings for dinner and

on your way out, grab a pound of house-made bacon and some chops for your own refrigerator. Where a chalkboard announcing the "Cuts Available Tonight" hangs just above the open kitchen. Where a Hawley Ranch lamb is delivered every Thursday and supplies both the meat counter and the dinner service. Where a quarter cow translates to Hanger and Prime Flat Iron, Smoked Brisket and Short Ribs. Where diners hear a butcher band saw fire up during the middle of dinner service. Where the good old boys can dine next to caricatures from Portlandia.

"We were doing these Americana takes on steakhouse night over at Simpatica," said chef-owner David Kreifels, referring to his other project with chefs and co-owners Jason Owens and Benjamin Dye. "They always sold out. We thought, we must be onto something. Then this location came along and it seemed like an ideal time."

Ideal it was. Not long after opening, Bon Appetit discovered the brilliance and charm of their reinvented design and in 2010 named Laurelhurst Market one of their Top 10 New Restaurants of the Year — a pretty stellar designation in a city whose food scene was just taking off.

Although their beef preparations are out of this world, Chef David says that it is his scallop dish that really reflects the sweet, salty, crunchy flavor profile he adores. Blood sausage, which is made right on site at the butcher shop, is seared and crumbled over a beautiful, thinly sliced seared sea scallop. In the summer it is served with a corn puree, lime butter sauce, beet chips and micro greens from Mizuno Farms.

Short Ribs are "hands-down" Chef David's favorite cut of beef and at Laurelhurst Market, treated a little different.

Chef David Kreifels' Tips for a Perfect Steak

Season and air-dry. The day before cooking, take the steak out of the packaging, season liberally with kosher salt and pepper, place it on a plate and put it in the fridge without a cover. The open air begins to dry the meat and will intensify its flavor.

Take the chill off. Before cooking, pull the meat out of the fridge, season again, and let it hang out on the counter for one hour.

Let it rest. When done, place your steak on a bed of parsley stems, fennel fronds, or whatever fresh herb you have laying around, hot side up (meaning whichever side was closest to the heat when pulled off). The hot air will rise and attract juices to the top of the meat where you want them. The herbs will add a final bit of flavor!

Finish with good salt. Buy some quality salt, like Jacobsen Sea Salt, and finish with just a sprinkle of crystals for one last bit of crunch and flavor.

Chef David lets them sit with a dry rub for a few days, then smokes them for six hours and serves with a boiled peanut chile.

Side dishes like Mac & Cheese with potato chip crust, Blistered Padron Peppers, Mom's Baked Beans, and Fried Cauliflower keeps things colorful, flavorful and exciting, yet familiar in the most comforting of ways.

Whether you're looking for a Tuesday night dinner, celebrating a special occasion with friends, in the market to buy deli meats and house-made sausages, or taking your father out for a beef-inspired feast—Laurelhurst Market is the indie steakhouse we've all been craving.

SMOKED BEEF BRISKET WITH OZARK BBQ SAUCE

(Serves 12-20)

This recipe is not labor intensive but does involve the use of a smoker for several hours. If you do not have access to a Traeger grill, any homemade smoke house would work great.

1   brisket - approx 12 lbs. We prefer a Wagyu brisket for its supreme marbling

FOR THE DRY RUB:

1   cup kosher salt
½   cup white sugar
¼   cup ground black pepper
⅛   cup paprika
⅛   cup onion powder
1   Tbs garlic powder
1   tsp cayenne

• Mix well. • Generously rub all over surface of brisket, working some of the seasoning into the meat creating a paste-like consistency. You may not need all the rub. The spices add to the "bark" that develops on the outer edge of the meat during the smoking process.

• Place rubbed brisket in fridge at least 24 hours – up to 3 days. • Set smoker to 200° and load with wood chips/pellets. Some smokers require you to replenish wood chips every few hours throughout the process. If your smoker doesn't go down to 200°, set as low as possible and reduce the time. • Leave in smoker for approximately 12-14 hours. It's really an internal temperature if 191° you're after.

• While the meat is smoking, prepare the BBQ sauce.

• Remove from smoker. • Let rest for at least a half hour.

If you are not serving immediately:
• Let rest for a half hour. • Wrap in plastic wrap and refrigerate. • When ready to serve, cut thick slices and sear in a pan.
• Coat with BBQ sauce and finish heating through in the oven.

OZARK BBQ SAUCE

1   cup onion, finely diced
4-5 cloves garlic, finely minced
⅓   cup canola oil
1   Tbs ground black pepper
1   Tbs kosher salt
1   Tbs dry mustard powder
1   Tbs paprika

1   Tbs chile powder
2   tsp ground cumin
1   tsp chile flakes
1¼   cups apple cider vinegar
½   cup Worcestershire
12   oz pilsner or lager style beer (Oly, Old German)
⅔   cup honey
½   cup brown sugar

• In a large, heavy bottom pot, sweat onion and garlic with canola oil until translucent

• Add spices including salt and cook over medium heat until spices begin to stick to bottom of pan. • Add remaining ingredients and bring to a simmer.

• Reduce heat • Maintain a simmer for one hour. Serve immediately or cool for later use.

JAMISON

🍴 SOMETIMES, WHEN ALL OF THE thoughtfully created pieces of a restaurant come together, the end result is a romantic story of time and place and people.

Such a story is told at Jamison, a restaurant in the heart of the Pearl District where thousands of feet of barn wood and vintage farm tools tastefully display the history of a family. Where food is hearty, simple and of the season. Where industrial design opens up to the natural urban beauty of Jamison Square Park.

Remember that a recipe is an interpretation. It's your job to experiment and play with it.

—Chef and Co-owner Gavin Ledson

Jamison is the vision of the essential Pearl District restaurant from Christopher Handford and Gavin Ledson (also of Davis Street Tavern, see page 36). Taking inspiration from the bounty that the Northwest has to offer, Jamison showcases the best in what Oregon prides itself: food and wine, along with warm, comfortable service and an unpretentious yet modern new American menu.

Chef Gavin Ledson's menu is made up of small shareable plates with a focus on in-season vegetables and flatbread creations, as well as several larger fully conceived plates. The idea stemmed from a desire to create a shareable feast that translates to the Northwest. The American version of tapas, you could say.

With a focus on vegetables, Jamison showcases the hard work of local farmers. Small plates like Roasted Cauliflower with anchovy butter and chile, Sauteed Foraged Mushrooms with shallot and sherry, and Charred Padron Peppers with olive oil and sea salt, these dishes show simple, thoughtful care. This is important to Chef Gavin, who grew up in Hawaii where raw and un-manipulated flavors were the cuisine of the day.

"I don't want to cover things up or make them something they're not," said Chef Gavin. "The farmers and ranchers do the really hard work. I just try not to mess it up."

Other small plates include a House Meat & Cheese Board, Charred Octopus, Tuna Tartare and Farro with Braised Oregon Lamb. Flatbreads are given Northwest inspiration with combinations such as Anjou pear with bleu cheese crema, walnut, sorrel, and lemon.

Larger plates include Cedar Plank Salmon with a brown sugar and cardamom rub, a duo of Seared Alaskan Halibut and Dungeness Crab dressed with a rhubarb beurre blanc when in season, and Seared Duck Breast with celery root, chanterelle and apple butter.

Brunch is also a highlight at Jamison where classics play out in fantastic form, and in the summer months, guests spill out onto what Christopher calls "the best patio in the city" overlooking the greenery and Sunday afternoon park play dates.

The true romance of the story, though, goes back to the history that Jamison has successfully encapsulated within its walls, quite literally. Much of the interior uses salvaged barn wood from a mill that was located not far from the restaurant. As the Schmidt Brothers Pellet Mill, the barns were integral to the local community for livestock, crops and timber. Jamison now reflects a concrete story of Northwest farming and timber culture—a story that connects so closely to the food it is known for creating in a quintessential Pearl District location.

CHARRED OCTOPUS

(Makes 4 Small Plates)

This is a great dish for entertaining as much of the work is done ahead of time and you can enjoy the company instead of slaving away while guests are there.

1	Spanish octopus, roughly 4-6 lbs, cleaned and gutted
1	head garlic
2	bay leaves
¼	cup whole black pepper
1	pint cherry tomatoes, tomatoes cut in half
1	navel orange, cut into segments (substitute blood oranges when available)
½	bunch cilantro, leaves picked
1	tsp spicy chile oil*

(*At Jamison they make their own by toasting chile de arbol pods in a very hot oven, then pureeing it with enough rice oil to blend. Store-bought chile oils will work also as the smell from roasting the dried pods is quite potent.)

Nicole Hart Photography

• Blanch the octopus in hot boiling water for 30 seconds. • Remove and allow the water to come back to a boil. • Blanch the octopus again for 30 more seconds and remove. • Repeat this once more for a total of three blanches.

• Lower the heat of the water to a gentle simmer and add the garlic, bay leaves, and black pepper. • Put octopus in the water and allow to simmer for roughly 1 hour and 15 minutes, or until the octopus is incredibly tender.

• Remove from the pot and immediately peel the outer membrane so the inner white is all that is remaining. Be careful, it will be really hot. Use multiple layers of gloves to withstand the hot temperature of the flesh without burning your own.

• Once it is peeled, chill for 4 hours and chop into bite sized pieces.

• When you are ready to serve your delicious octopus, put a sauté pan on the heat and get it as hot as possible.

• In a bowl, combine the chile oil, octopus, and tomato and add it to the pan. Be sure to keep the pan moving as the octopus can stick. You are looking for bits of charred octopus and texture at this point. It is already cooked.

• Remove from the pan and add the orange segments and cilantro to the octopus. • Season with salt and pepper, and enjoy!

EAT: AN OYSTER BAR

TOBIAS HOGAN AND Ethan Powell opened EaT: An Oyster Bar in 2008, just after the Lehman Brothers went down.

"You picked a crazy time to open a restaurant," said their friends and patrons.

Tobias acknowledges that it was crazy, but the pair certainly did not plan to open their first restaurant in the midst of global financial upheaval. So despite the twiddling-thumbs atmosphere of the N. Williams neighborhood space during those early, empty weeks, giving up was never an option.

They believed that their concept, an egalitarian oyster bar serving raw oysters, Cajun and Creole, would one day attract people looking for good food for not a lot of money.

And they were right. Eventually, the place filled up with oyster-hungry Portlanders on the search for an affordable,

Jason Staats

comfortable and friendly meal. They also found Cajun Creole classics such as Étouffée, Gumbo and Jambalaya, not to mention a stellar brunch with Shrimp & Grits, Soft Shell Crab Po'boy, Beignets and live New Orleans jazz every Sunday.

"We wanted to create an oyster-eating culture in Portland," said Ethan.

That they did. With a second restaurant, Parish, now open and located in the Pearl District (see page 30), they serve 800-1,000 dozen oysters each week.

Because they work direct with Northwest farms, the oysters are as fresh and sustainable as they come. If originating in an Oregon farm, the oysters that hit your plate at EaT have been out of the water just 3-4 hours, said Ethan. This quick turnaround ensures that an oyster at EaT holds on to its Merroir, its unique flavor profile based on location — the taste of Pacific Northwest waters in its truest sense.

If you crave a glass of bubbles with your oysters on the half-shell, you'll find it at EaT. Although casual in design and atmosphere, the bar serves a nice selection of Champagne alongside cans of Olympia beer.

If you're not an oyster lover, there is more great food to be had, including: Shrimp Étouffée, Fried Okra, Collard Greens, Blackened Catfish, Cajun Barbecue Shrimp, Fried Frog Legs and three types of Gumbo. "The Finale," aka dessert, offers Southern Bread Pudding drizzled with a house-made whiskey sauce and House-made Pecan Pie.

But you can't deny the truth as stated by Jonathan Swift and quoted by Ethan: "He was a bold man that first ate an oyster."

Whether it's your first or 500th oyster, we urge you to be bold at EaT.

> *We wanted to create an oyster-eating culture in Portland.*
>
> —Ethan Powell, chef and co-owner

DUCK GUMBO

Roux Careful

When you're cooking your roux, you want to look for a dark, toasty smell, almost like popcorn. Be careful—if you go too far and burn it, you can't save it.

—Ethan Powell, chef and co-owner

EaT serves this Gumbo with their house-made chili garlic vinegar and house-made fermented chile sauces for an extra kick!

1	cup duck fat roux
1	whole duck (Muscovy hen)
2	cups yellow onion, diced
1	cup green bell pepper, diced
1	cup celery stalks, diced
1	Tbs garlic, minced
1	cup Roma tomato, diced
3	cups okra (sliced into ½" rounds)
8	cups duck stock
2¼	tsp cayenne pepper
½	tsp thyme leaves (fresh)
1	large bay leaf
2	Tbs salt

DUCK FAT ROUX

1	cup duck fat
1	cup all purpose flour

• In a heavy bottom pot over a medium flame, melt the duck fat and slowly whisk in the flour to avoid clumping.
• Continue stirring constantly to avoid scorching. Keep stirring and adjust temperature down if the roux begins to brown too quickly. Keep cooking and stirring until desired darkness.
• Quickly cool by pouring roux into a heat resistant container resting in an ice bath and store, or use immediately to make your Gumbo.

DUCK STOCK

• Butcher the duck, by taking the breast and leg/thigh off the bones and set aside. • Roast the bones in the oven at 450° until dark brown but not burned (about 20-30 min). • Place your bones in a stock pot with cold water, 1 onion quartered, one large carrot roughly chopped, one celery rib roughly chopped, one bay leaf and ten pepper corns. • Bring everything to a boil; reduce to a simmer skimming any fat that rises to the top. • Cook for 3-4 hours and reserve for use in your Gumbo.

DUCK CONFIT

• In a casserole dish, cover the duck legs in melted duck fat, place aromatic herbs under the legs with a few garlic cloves, cover with foil and cook in the oven at 300º for approximately 2 hours.
• Remove the legs from the fat and allow to cool. • For service, warm duck legs in a hot oven. • To crisp the skin, put the pan under the broiler on high, being careful not to burn. • Serve on top of the finished Gumbo.

DUCK BREAST

• Season the breast with Hungarian paprika, salt, pepper and a touch of cayenne and smoke for 3 hours at 275°.
• Allow to cool until you can handle and chop into ½" cubes.

GUMBO

• Prepare the roux, and while hot, sauté the onion, celery and green pepper until soft, add the garlic and continue to sauté until aromatic. • Then add the diced tomato. Continue to stir so nothing burns. • At this point you can add the okra and then slowly add your warm stock stirring constantly to avoid clumps. • Once all the ingredients are incorporated into the stock, put in the rest of your seasoning and add the chopped duck breast. • Bring everything to a boil, but do not allow the gumbo to come to a rolling boil. • Reduce heat to a simmer and allow the Gumbo to cook for three hours.

FOR SERVICE

• Steam some heirloom long grain rice according to directions. • Ladle gumbo into a shallow serving bowl with a scoop of rice in the middle. • Top with the finished duck confit leg and garnish with scallions or chives sliced on the bias.

MISS DELTA

WHEN MISS DELTA reopened under new ownership in August of 2012, you really couldn't judge what its future would hold by the size of the only smoker this southern comfort food joint owned.

Borrowed from co-owner Nick Weitz's personal stash and placed in a back alley of their Mississippi space, the tiny smoker could fit just two pork butts at a time.

"Yeah, we ran that thing into the ground pretty quick," laughed chef and co-owner Marcus Oliver.

What followed in the weeks and months ahead would help secure a much larger smoker for the restaurant—neighborhood enthusiasm, a refined menu, two dedicated and passionate owners, desire and care, a crew that truly loves great southern food, and quite possibly the best 10-hour smoked brisket this side of the Delta.

Yep. Miss Delta now has a beauty of a smoker, a sleek and shiny Yoder model that symbolizes the huge success the past year and a half has earned them, and actually fits enough brisket and pulled pork to keep their southern-soul fans from the neighborhood and beyond well fed.

Marcus, with southern roots and the key to his Alabama grandmother's banana pudding recipe, and Nick, with a background in restaurant development—both lifelong friends—had one thought when they first considered the purchase of Miss Delta.

"This style of food, this cross-section of Mississippi soul food—yeah, we thought, we could really nail this," said Marcus.

And nail it they did. This is not the Miss Delta of years gone by. This is a more focused, refined and flavorful Miss Delta. Fried chicken just like your grandmother's with a choice of white or dark meat. A buttery, rich Étouffée done right with seafood, bell pepper, celery and green onion. Po Boys on French baguette with Miss Delta sauce and all the fixings and your choice of pulled pork, fried or blackened catfish, fried oyster, shrimp or crawfish.

They've also teamed up with Portland Pepper Sauce Co. to bottle their own recipe of hot sauce and designed an authentic Andouille sausage with the help of Portland powerhouse butcher Olympic Provisions, both of which are now available for purchase at Miss Delta.

And don't forget about Grandma's Banana Pudding with vanilla wafers and whipped cream. Yes, that Grandma. Marcus' grandmother, originally of Florence, Alabama, has left a major southern soul mark on Miss Delta, as has the greater idea of family spirit that this restaurant embodies.

If you take a close look at the dining room walls, you'll notice a nod to both Nick's and Marcus' families. In an effort to give the space a more personal feel, they blew up old family photos onto canvases that are now spread all over the wall. Each photo has a little story behind it — even the photo of Elvis, who unfortunately, the boys say, isn't family.

And isn't that the real heart of soul cooking? Family. Heart. And a whole lot of love. The smoker? Well, it sure is nice, but for this place, it's secondary.

Southern Soul Food

Jambalaya is a rice dish descended from Spanish Paella. It makes a great one-pot meal for any occasion. Miss Delta's version is full of meat, seafood, diced tomatoes and bold flavors with the added bonus of Olympic Provisions Andouille sausage and Miss Delta hot sauce.

JAMBALAYA

(Serves 6-8)

Feel free to add more hot sauce or cayenne than calls for if you want to spice it up even more. Serve with warm cornbread and lots of hot sauce on the side.

- 4 Andouille sausages, split lengthwise and sliced 1/2 inch thick
- 2 lb boneless/skinless chicken thighs, thinly sliced
- 2 Tbs minced garlic
- 1 yellow onion, julienned
- 1 green bell pepper, diced
- 1 red bell pepper, diced
- 6 cups diced tomatoes in juice
- 3 cups chicken stock (preferable roasted at home)
- 2 bay leaves
- 2 Tbs Miss Delta hot sauce
- 2 Tbs fresh parsley, rough chopped
- 1 Tbs smoked paprika
- 1 Tbs garlic granules
- 1 Tbs kosher salt
- 1 Tbs dried chives
- 2 tsp dried thyme
- 2 tsp fresh ground black pepper
- 2 tsp onion powder
- 2 tsp dried oregano
- 2 tsp cayenne pepper

Photos Deborah Buchanan

- 2 tsp chile powder
- 2 cups small shrimp
- 6 cups par-cooked long grain white rice

• Heat 2 Tbs extra virgin olive/canola blend oil, onion, garlic and bell pepper in a large pot and cook, stirring occasionally, until softened slightly. • Add Andouille sausage and chicken. • Cook for 5-7 minutes, stirring occasionally.

• Add the rest of the ingredients except

for shrimp and rice and bring to a boil. • Reduce to medium and simmer until liquid reduces slightly and flavors develop. Taste and adjust salt and pepper, if needed.

• Add the shrimp, stir and cook for 5 minutes. • Add rice and stir to combine. Cook, stirring, until rice is softened and shrimp are fully cooked.

• Scoop into bowls and garnish with lots of chopped green onion. (Optional: Add two or three blackened prawns on top!)

BISTRO MARQUEE

Alison Jones The Screen Door

🍴 GARY KNESKI AND LESLIE PALMER, the husband and wife team behind Thirst Wine Bar & Bistro, said they really weren't looking to open a second restaurant, which is usually exactly what someone says before they're about to open another restaurant.

Enter Bistro Marquee, Thirst's younger downtown sibling. Appealing to Portland's theater crowd and downtown office workers alike, Bistro Marquee is the place to go for simple flavors, outstanding wine and delicious desserts.

Award-winning chef and Portland Iron chef winner Rick Widmayer, formerly of the Screen Door, has brought a refined approach to classic French and New American cuisine highlighting local meats, seafood and amazing produce.

Lunches are simple and flavorful, allowing downtown business guests to finish a midday meal in under an hour with salads, sandwiches, burgers, and a French onion soup showcasing Willamette Valley Gouda. The Crispy Cornmeal Fried Yaquina Bay Oyster Po'Boy is a favorite, as are the Half Pound Dry-Aged House Ground Burgers with add-ons such as a fried egg, caramelized onions, Applewood smoked bacon, Beecher's cheddar, crispy onion straws, sautéed mushrooms, crispy pork belly and crumbled blue cheese. The burgers are served on a brioche roll or a gluten-free bun.

At dinner, the menu offers soups, salads, small and large plates, and handmade pastas. Pan Seared Salmon, Crispy Skin Draper Valley Chicken, Duck Confit and Braised Lamb Shank stand next to handmade Orecchiette, Portland Creamery Goat Cheese Ravioli with hazelnut brown butter sauce, and Stroganoff with homemade wide egg noodles.

Perhaps the crowning winner is found at Happy Hour when Chef Rick makes his famous fried chicken. Served as crispy bone-in pieces, the chicken is brined in sweet tea before frying and served with skillet cornbread and smoked honey. The Happy Hour at Bistro Marquee runs late, from 4pm-7pm, a fact that makes downtown office workers more than happy.

Because of their close proximity to Keller Auditorium (most guests can make the trek in about 25 seconds, said Leslie), Bistro Marquee offers prix fixe dinners before most shows. Three beautiful courses make for the perfect pre-show gathering with friends.

You'll also find Thirst's famous Sangria that Leslie decided to export to Bistro Marquee. She developed the recipe herself years ago and the now signature drink has received great fanfare ever since. Made with red wine, fresh

fruit and a few "super-secret ingredients," it's a refreshing, beautiful drink that Bistro Marquee guests know and love.

On most days, you'll find Leslie at the front door greeting guests. The owner-operated feel of Bistro Marquee is genuine, and that translates to the staff. So the next time you're downtown and need a cocktail or a bite to eat, look for the greenery-covered awning, wicker patio tables and free valet parking with validation after 5pm. Leslie has a seat waiting just for you.

Chef's Choice

Bistro Marquee is the proud home of Chef Rick Widmayer. If you miss his famous Happy Hour Chicken, be sure to order his favorite burger, topped with Beecher's Cheddar, Pork Belly, Crispy Onion Straws, and Caper Aioli.

MOUSSE DE CHOCOLAT BLANCO
on Gluten Free Chocolate Torte

This recipe is in care of Bistro Marquee Pastry Chef Justin Taylor

(Serves 8)

TORTE

½ lb dark chocolate
½ cup butter
¾ cup sugar
4 eggs
½ cup cocoa
¼ tsp salt
½ tsp vanilla

• Melt chocolate and butter in double boiler. • Stir in sugar. • Whisk in eggs one at a time, sift in cocoa. • Pipe into four 4 oz ramekins placed on a cookie sheet. • Bake at 350° for 30 minutes. • Let cool on baking rack.

MOUSSE

3 oz whipping cream
1 egg yolk
½ vanilla bean
7 oz white chocolate
10 oz whipping cream
1 tsp gelatin

• Cream together yolk, vanilla, and 3 oz whipping cream in a double boiler until temperature reaches 160°.

• In a separate bowl activate gelatin with 1 Tbs cold water. • Add that to the yolk cream mixture.

• In a food processor pulse the white chocolate until finely ground. • Then slowly add the yolk cream mixture and continue pulsing until creamy smooth.

• Beat 10 oz whipping cream until stiff peaks form and fold into white chocolate mix.

GANACHE

6 oz dark chocolate
¾ oz cold butter
4 oz whipping cream
2 oz alcohol of choice (Grand Marnier works well)
Powdered almonds

• In double boiler place cold butter and chocolate, melt until smooth.

• In a pan bring whipping cream to a boil and temper into chocolate.

• Remove your tortes from ramekins.
• Cut each in half across the middle, leaving you with 8 spheres. • Using 2½-inch width pieces of plastic wrap, wrap bottom and sides of tortes and fit back into ramekins so they rest at the bottom of the cylinder with extra plastic wrap falling from sides. • Fill cylinders almost to the brim with your mousse mixture.

• Refrigerate for 1 hour.

• Pulling the plastic, gently lift the tortes out of the ramekins, keeping the mousse in its form. • Smooth it all around the edges.

• Using a ladle, pour 2 oz of ganache on top of each cake so it drips lightly around the edges. • Finish with powdered almonds and chill until serving.

DAN & LOUIS OYSTER BAR

ONE HUNDRED AND SEVEN YEARS
celebrating the Northwest oyster. There is more family history wrapped up in this restaurant than any other in all of Portland.

Dan & Louis Oyster Bar opened in 1907, right around the time that this now iconic image was taken of the restaurant's original proprietor Louis C. Wachsmuth (far left). Out on the sidewalk between 2nd and 3rd on Ankeny Street, he was surrounded by a group of burly men, sacks of Oregon oysters and boxes full of live Dungeness crabs destined for a big, briny crab pot inside his wholesale and retail seafood store where oyster cocktails were also served.

As one might glean from the photograph, Louis was no stranger to seafood. His father, Meinert Wachsmuth, was a seaman. Mienert sailed around the Horn seven times and to almost every port in the world before settling down in 1865 to work on the oyster schooners plying their way between San Francisco and the oyster rich bays of Oregon and Washington. Meinert and his family moved to Shoalwater Bay in 1881 and took up squatter's rights on oyster beds. Louis loved growing up around his father and brothers on the oyster farm. He developed a life long curiosity for the succulent bivalves that would follow him to Portland.

This tradition and intrinsic connection to the sea was what propelled Louis to become a successful restaurant owner in Portland. That, and a piping hot bowl of oyster stew served on a cold, wintry day. Made with right-out-of-the-shell oysters added to a pot of creamy rich milk, butter and seasoning, the stew drew a crowd that lined up around the block. Louis was forced to enlarge his operation, becoming a true restaurant and oyster house not long after. He also started the Oregon Oyster Farm in Yaquina Bay to supply his now booming business.

Today, Dan & Louis Oyster Bar is run by Louis' great-grandson Meinert Keoni Wachsmuth (who goes by Keoni). In many ways, it is just the same as it was in the early 20th century—working with local family-owned companies to maintain the highest quality and standard of service.

"We really pride ourselves on sourcing the best oysters

available," said Keoni. "It's about building relationships with local oyster farmers that share the same passion and love for the oyster."

Of course, oyster farming has come a long way over the last century, and Dan & Louis Oyster Bar is now serving their guests some of the most prized varieties in the Northwest with greater ease. Hama Hama Oyster Company in Lilliwaup, Washington is one of their partners. This family-owned operation has been farming oysters and clams on the Olympic Peninsula for more than five generations and collects some of the most delicious shellfish in the world including the Block B, Blue Pool, Seacow and the wild-grown Hama Hama oysters. The Block B is the premier variety and Dan & Louis Oyster Bar is the only restaurant in the state of Oregon and one of only five in the country with the Block B on the menu.

In addition to raw oysters on the half shell, you'll also find Dungeness crab, steamer clams, grilled prawns, fried seafood cakes, Oyster Rockefeller, clam chowder, grilled wild salmon, pan seared scallops, fried oysters, grilled steak and pork chops, and yes, that oyster stew that Louis made famous over a century ago.

It's about building relationships with local oyster farmers that share the same passion and love for the oyster.

—**Keoni Wachsmuth, owner**

The fact that Dan & Louis Oyster Bar has been handed down from father to son for five generations says a lot about this family, this restaurant and the continuing history that has placed this address on the register as a Portland landmark. You can bet wife Michelle and children Kai, Hana and Kaleo know a thing or two about oysters.

DAN & LOUIS OYSTER ROCKEFELLER

1	dozen 3"-4" fresh in-shell Pacific oysters
1	Tbs pepper bacon, diced
1	Tbs shallots, minced
1	tsp garlic, minced
1	cup spinach, chopped
2	Tbs white wine
1	tsp white wine vinegar
1	tsp lemon juice
¼	cup heavy cream
¼	tsp Pernod
5	drops Tabasco
5	drops Worcestershire
1	oz Gruyere cheese, grated
	Salt and pepper to taste

• In a sauté pan wilt the spinach.
• Remove from pan, cool and squeeze out extra juice. • Set the spinach aside and discard the juice.
• In a sauté pan render bacon on medium heat, until the bacon has browned just lightly. • Add shallots and garlic, then sauté until lightly translucent. • Add wine, vinegar and lemon juice. • Reduce by three-quarters. • Add the heavy cream. • Reduce by one-quarter. • Add the Tabasco, Worcestershire and Pernod. • Reduce by one-quarter. • Season with salt and pepper to taste. • Remove from heat and let the mixture cool slightly.

• Fold Gruyere cheese into the mixture, saving a little to sprinkle on top at the end. • Cool to room temperature. • Fold the spinach into mixture and set aside.

• Preheat oven to 425°. • Bake oysters cup side down for 7 minutes or until they pop open. • Remove the flat shell, put the spinach mixture on the oysters, and sprinkle some cheese on top.

• Turn the oven to broil and broil the oysters until the cheese lightly browns.
• Serve the oysters on a bed of rock salt with a slice of lemon.

KARAM LEBANESE & SYRIAN CUISINE

Not to the surprise of everyone at the table, the guest refused. It was too grand, too personal, too much. She couldn't possibly accept. But to Majdolen, it wasn't even a question. You give to others. You are kind and welcoming. You are generous.

Generous. This is a word and spirit that runs deep through Majdolen's personal identity as well as her family line. It was her aunts and uncles who first purchased the restaurant in 1988. After several iterations, they eventually named it Karam, which is the Arabic translation of the word "generous." Majdolen took over the restaurant in 2011 when her family retired to their village in Lebanon.

This thread of generosity is in every room of the restaurant, from the way Majdolen greets guests at the door to the way she recognizes birthdays. Men are given a birthday vest. Women are given a grand velvet princess hat. They pose for pictures that are published on Facebook with heartfelt best wishes. Whatever has brought you to Karam, celebration or not, it's as if you've joined a good friend in their own private home.

Born in Syria of Syrian and Lebanese descent, Majdolen learned from a very early age to be hospitable. She also learned how to cook.

She worked in the kitchen as a young girl beside her mother, aunts and grandmother in Syria. Preparing for a weekly family gathering was a tradition among these Syrian and Lebanese women, and they inspired the young Majdolin to watch and learn. They made giant maamoul, a traditional Easter and Christmas dessert filled with

> *Ingredients don't make a dish special; there must be love and a passion for cooking to bring a dish to perfection.*
>
> —Majdolen Khouri,
> chef and owner

AT KARAM, GENEROSITY COMES
from the heart.

And perhaps the best example of this truth involves a pair of earrings.

One night during dinner service, a guest complimented Karam owner and chef Majdolen Khouri on her earrings.

Majdolen then did something that she says many Americans would find perplexing.

She immediately said, "Okay, they're yours," took the earrings out of her own ears, placed them on a platter, and presented them to her guest who was celebrating a birthday that night.

SUPER FOOD

Majdolen chose to share this recipe for Mujaddara because it is friendly to all diets. Vegetarian, vegan and gluten free, it is hearty and healthy. You can use brown or green lentils. Find them in the bulk section of your local market.

Lentils are considered a super food—high in fiber, protein, vitamin B, and iron, and when combined with rice complete a high-protein dish.

dates, walnuts or pistachios, to be shared with neighbors and friends for days on end. They made traditional baba ganoush, kafka, artichoke stew and pita bread.

"You can't help but learn something when you watch your mother cook," she said.

And learn she did. She quickly became the family's favorite cook, whipping up dishes that pleased both herself and guests that popped in for a visit.

That family tradition continues at Karam, where customers say their yearning for a Lebanese mamma's home-cooked lunch is satisfied. The real treat comes from steaming fresh pita bread, which arrives still warm and puffy from the oven, perfect for dipping into their fantastic hummus or sopping up broths from complex stews. Majdolen is happy to announce that they now offer gluten-free pita as well as the traditional recipe. The menu

has many dishes that you won't see elsewhere, including three preparations of goat, fresh pumpkin kibbeh, and molokhie—a traditional layered dish with bread, rice, cilantro, mallow leaves and lamb.

Because of its importance in the diet, a saying in the Eastern Arab world is, 'A hungry man would be willing to sell his soul for a dish of mujaddara.'

For a young woman that moved to Portland and opened a food and catering kiosk at the Portland Saturday Market, taking over the family business at Karam was "a dream come true."

You'll see that spark of love and generosity each and every time you visit Majdolen at Karam.

MUJADDARA (ARABIC LENTIL RICE)

(Serves 4)

- ¾ cup of lentils
- ½ cup of rice
- 2 whole onions, sliced
- 3 Tbs of olive oil
- 1 tsp of cumin
- 3 Tbs of olive oil
- 1 Tbs of chopped fresh parsley

• Boil rice and 1 cup of water in a small pan. • Turn heat to low and cook for about 25 minutes or until done.

• Heat olive oil in a sauté pan. • Add both onions and sauté until they turn golden in color. • Add cumin, stir and set aside.

• Place lentils in 2 cups of water and boil until ready. (10-15 min)

• Cook the rice and lentils with half of the golden onions on low temperature.

• After mixed and warmed through, place the second half of golden onions to the top of the lentil rice and sprinkle with parsley.

Photos Jason Staats

BAR MINGO

🍴 CHEF JERRY HUISINGA HAS QUITE
possibly, made more pasta than anyone else in the entire
city of Portland.

Over the course of his nearly 30 years as a chef in this
city, he has made pasta most every day. At Genoa, where for
22 years he was part of a group of passionate "home cooks"
who were at the forefront of Portland's changing food scene.
At Caffe Mingo where he perfected his pasta making skills.
And now at Bar Mingo where his Marcella Hazan-driven
philosophy and own personal style come together to the
point of perfection.

It is a basic pasta recipe in the Bar Mingo kitchen, said
Jerry, made just like your grandmother did, with a hand
crank, dish towels and
clotheslines for drying. There
is care, there is craftsmanship,
and there are five to six
different kinds made each
and every day. Egg tagliatelle,
pappardelle, ravioli, lasagna
noodles, chitarra and
tonnarelli destined for
simple, full-flavored sauces.

*Jerry has cooked at The
James Beard House in
Manhattan and also
studied with his mentor
Marcella Hazan at The
French Culinary Institute.*

"We are known for our
pastas. We take a lot of care. No dry pasta here," said Jerry.

Jerry's knowledge of regional Italian food flourished
during his time at Genoa. Together with his fellow kitchen
crew, he contributed to the growing reputation of authentic
Italian food that Genoa enjoyed in its heyday. During this
time Jerry was honored to cook a Columbus Day dinner
at The James Beard House in Manhattan. He also studied
with his mentor Marcella Hazan at The French Culinary
Institute.

An advocate of simply prepared, full-flavored food that
honors the main ingredients at the height of their season,

Meatball 101

*Don't over-mix your meatballs. Mix them gently until
the ingredients just come together. If you go too far, your
meatballs will be tough.*

—Jerry Huisinga, chef

Jerry's goal at Bar Mingo is to bring great taste and good
value to the customers while channeling simple Italian home
cooking.

"We have these clean lines in design and concept here at
Bar Mingo," said owner Mike Cronan. "Things are simple,
and youthful and fun. And then Jerry sneaks up on you with

his food and damn! You realize that this is really great food."

Part of the Bar Mingo concept, "a new way to eat Italian"
where the main ingredients are good food and good people,
and the preparation is lighter and easier, is exactly what drew
Jerry to the restaurant.

"I really like the casual aspect of Bar Mingo," said Jerry.
"As a chef, I'm not isolated from the customers. I try to be
welcoming and an easy person to approach and I love to give
my guests cooking tips."

This is very good news for home cooks everywhere.
Pull up a chair, order a drink and a small plate followed by a
dish of pasta. Then be on the lookout for a friendly looking
white-haired chef in dark glasses. He holds the secret you're
looking for, so if you grab his attention, listen, and hold on to
his advice like you would that of your Italian grandmother.

LAMB MEATBALLS IN TOMATO SAUCE
flavored with Oregano and Mint

(Serves 8)

Make a big pot of this sauce and then use the leftovers for pasta and pizza. It is also delicious layered over polenta squares and then baked with a piece of fresh mozzarella.

LAMB MEATBALLS

⅔	cup milk
2	slices hearty bread, crusts removed
2	lbs ground lamb
¼	cup onion, finely chopped
2	Tbs Italian parsley, finely chopped
¼	tsp nutmeg, grated
2	eggs
⅓	cup Parmesan cheese, grated
2	Tbs olive oil
	Salt and pepper
	Dry breadcrumbs for coating the meatballs

• Put the milk and bread into a saucepan and bring to a boil. • Mash the bread with a fork and blend it uniformly into the milk. • Set aside and let cool before proceeding with the next step.

• In a mixing bowl, put the ground lamb, onion, parsley, egg, nutmeg, Parmesan cheese, oil, the bread and milk mixture, and salt and pepper to taste. • Mix everything thoroughly but gently by hand.

• Gently, without squeezing, shape the mixture into small round balls about 1½" in diameter. • Roll the meatballs in the dry breadcrumbs to coat. • Refrigerate while making the sauce.

TOMATO SAUCE

1	onion, chopped
3	cloves garlic, chopped
¼	cup fresh mint, chopped
1	Tbs dry oregano
½	cup white wine
2	28 oz cans whole tomatoes

• In a heavy bottomed pot, heat 3 Tbs olive oil until hot. • Add the chopped onions and garlic and sauté until beginning to soften. • Add the fresh mint and dry oregano. • Add the wine and continue to cook until the wine has all but disappeared. • Add the canned tomatoes and bring to a boil. • Lower to a simmer and cook sauce until it is thickened. You may want to put the sauce through a food mill if you want a smoother sauce.

• Meanwhile, heat 3 Tbs olive oil in a frying pan over medium heat until hot. • Add the meatballs and fry, turning to brown on all sides. You may have to do this in batches. *Take care not to crowd the meatballs.* • Keep meatballs warm until all the meatballs are browned.

• Place the meatballs into an ovenproof casserole with as much sauce as you need to cover the balls halfway. • Place in a 400° oven for about 10 minutes to finish cooking.

FOR GARNISH

¼	cup mint, roughly chopped
¼	cup Italian parsley, roughly chopped
½	cup ground pecorino Romano cheese

• To serve, dust liberally with grated pecorino Romano cheese and sprinkle with chopped fresh mint and oregano.

SEATTLE

You cannot begin to understand the food in Seattle without first thinking about water. Whether it is the type that famously falls from a rain-soaked sky or the type that fills the surrounding Pacific Ocean and Puget Sound, water is central to the identity of this city.

In the areas surrounding Seattle, water brings life to tasty seafood like Dungeness crab and clams and salmon. It also brings life to gifts from the land like truffles and chanterelles, apple trees and grape vines, livestock grasses and cheese. Water is a source for life, and in this city, it gives birth to food and ingredient like no other.

Long known for a coffee culture that flows through the streets and veins of its inhabitants, Seattle is often touted for its love of the java bean. And it's true—perhaps because of or in spite of the rain—the independent cafes as well as some of the nation's most famous coffee companies are found everywhere. But there is so much more to Seattle than fantastically brewed coffee.

From the fish throwers to the farmers that fill Pike Place Market, the country's oldest farmers market, Seattle has at its fingertips a bounty of fresh, local and sustainable ingredients with which to cook. Pair that with a collection of premier chefs and you have a recipe for something intensely magical—a restaurant scene that is mature, abundant and intimately reflective of this place.

In Seattle, chefs are able to bring thoughtful approaches to the beautiful resources they are surrounded by, including many who have become legendary in the world of food and dining. Increasingly though, diners are also enjoying small chef-inspired restaurants in areas that were once dominated by corporate chains and big restaurant business. Now, chefs are finding heart in communities where local ownership and locally inspired cuisine win with refreshing flavors and unique experiences.

Water, of course, also has a huge effect on the geography of this city. A major port, Seattle has long been a large thoroughfare for people and products from Asia. As such, there is a wonderful influence of Asian cuisine and culture. Warm broths, noodles, and traditionally intense and savory and bold flavors are found throughout the city and influence cuisine from authentic to fusion styles.

Seattle, at its heart, is an extraordinary combination of nature and culture. It is a place where everyone belongs, where everyone reaps the benefits of lush lands and independent, creative thought.

So whether you call it Seatown or Emerald City, Seattle, with its incomparable access to fresh, local and international ingredients, is one of the greatest food cities in America.

Photos John Granen

POPPY

TWO WEEKS AFTER GETTING BACK from a culinary tour of India, Chef Jerry Traunfeld had a revelation.

The trip was supposed to be research for his third cookbook, but upon return, the project refused to come together as planned. One day he was hit with a vision: A new restaurant concept in Capitol Hill called Poppy. He thought of the name, he thought of the design, he thought of the location, he thought of the menu—he thought of everything all in that one moment.

His inspiration came clearly from the thalis he had feasted on while in India. Thalis are platters that hold a variety of dishes, often including vegetables, soup, salad, legumes and pickle. He enjoyed these traditional platters all over the country. From the south, where they were beautiful and refreshing with tropical flavors of coconut, to the north, where they were spicy and strong and full of hearty legumes, Jerry was delighted with this style of eating. He thought it a unique idea to borrow the thali to present his own style of northwest cooking.

"I found it to be such a wonderful way to nourish yourself," said Jerry.

And surprisingly, no one had taken this concept and translated it to American dining, or more specifically, northwest cuisine. Jerry, the James Beard award-winning chef from the wildly popular Herbfarm, was onto something and in 2008, Poppy opened to great success.

An easy way to describe Poppy is a modern northwest tasting menu served all at once. But at thoughtful inspection,

it's so much more. The "Today's Thali" menu offers six thali selections each containing a combination of six small dishes. The ingredients and preparations change seasonally, but to paint a picture let's pretend to order the Copper River Coho Salmon w/ Savoy Cabbage and Matsutake. Inside this single platter, built for one person, you'll find a galeux d'eysines pumpkin soup; a dish of radicchio, apple and black olive salad; a Swiss chard and oregano gratin; herbed cranberry

beans and maitake mushrooms; pickled figs; and nigella-poppy naan. The platter is interactive and spirited from start to finish—a feast for the eyes, the nose, and most certainly the taste buds as fresh-cut herbs and spices pop and surprise around every corner of the platter.

Desserts are also served thali style, with a choice of Dessert (small cakes, tortes, custards, panna cotta) or Ice Cream. Or you can splurge and share the "Sweet Thali for Two" which comes with one dessert, one ice cream and a sprinkling of poppycorn, nutter-butter squares, apricot and black tea pâtes de fruit, and chocolate passion-fruit marshmallows.

The dishes themselves are also a beautiful part of the

CAPITOL HILL • SEATTLE

experience. In India, traditional thalis are served on stainless steel platters and dishes. In an effort to modernize this aesthetic, Jerry brought in mid-century modern ceramics from Sausalito, California. Warm hues and unique textures come together to tell a story of color and flavor.

The author of *The Herbfarm Cookbook* and *The Herbal Kitchen: Cooking with Fragrance*, Jerry is an icon of the American herb garden. He continues to tend garden at

Herb Advice

"Grow your own herbs and cut them fresh whenever you can. The flavor is so much better. It really will change the way you cook."
—Chef Jerry Traunfeld

Poppy of course, in a 500 square-foot space where more than two-dozen herb varieties including lovage, lemon verbena and scented geranium spill out of rustic boxes and giant pots. The fresh-cut herbs are a mainstay in the Poppy kitchen during the summer months, and wane during the winter when spices become more appealing to Jerry's profile. The garden, one of the most magical spaces on Capitol Hill, opens for dinner service in the warm months via six poppy-red colored patio tables.

This might be an assumption on our part, but we're fairly certain that fans of Poppy are thankful that Jerry's trip to India took him down a different path than originally planned. We're also fairly certain that he will eventually write that third cookbook.

ROASTED DELICATA SQUASH
with Chanterelles and Apricot

(Serves 6)

This dish can be served as part of a thali or a large main dish to serve the table.

SPICE MIX

1½	tsp cumin seed
¾	tsp ground cinnamon
	Pinch saffron
¾	tsp powdered ginger
¼	tsp black peppercorn
	Pinch cayenne pepper or red pepper flake
½	tsp ground turmeric
¼	tsp fresh ground nutmeg
	Zest of ¼ lemon
2	tsp kosher salt
2	delicata squash
1	red onion
3	Tbs olive oil
½	lb chanterelle mushrooms, cleaned, or substitute other fresh mushrooms like shiitake, maitake or crimini
¾	cup dried apricot halves, sliced

• Preheat the oven to 425° in convection oven or 450° if in conventional oven.

• Put all the ingredients for the spice mix in a rotary coffee mill and grind until fine.

• Peel the squash with a vegetable peeler, cut them in half and use a spoon to scrape out the seeds. • Slice in ½" thick half circles. • Peel the onion, cut it in half from root to tip and slice it thickly again from root to tip. • Tear the chanterelles into pieces if they are large.

• Toss the squash, onion, oil, chanterelles and spice mix together in a large shallow baking dish. • Bake uncovered, stirring several times, until the squash begins to brown, about 20 minutes.

• Add the apricots, cover, and return to the oven until the squash is very tender, another 10 to 15 minutes.

• Serve with couscous or a whole grain, such as faro or quinoa.

CHAN

BORN IN KOREA, raised in Alaska, a son of restaurant owners who swore he'd never follow in his parents' footsteps, moved to Seattle with his new wife and a business degree. Looking for an investment in their future, they purchased Bacco Cafe, an Italian café and juice bar in the heart of Pike Place Market. He soon realized he needed more knowledge to make Bacco successful and enrolled in culinary school, taking classes at night after the juice bar closed.

He learned the fundamentals of French and Italian cooking. He worked 15-hour days, just like his parents, fusing Pacific Northwest cuisine with Italian flair in dishes such as Ratatouille with Eggs, Dungeness Crab Omelet and Brioche French Toast.

He thought about his childhood in Korea—his family,

Executive Chef Heong Soon Park (known as Chef Park).

So, in 2012, despite achieving great success at Bacco Café (though void of recipes from an Italian grandmother) Park and his wife took a second leap of faith and opened another restaurant, right next to Bacco. This one would flourish in a different way, bearing new growth on old roots. They named it Chan.

The concept of Chan is modern traditional Korean fusing the very best of local and fresh Northwest products. You will find a full bar with giant bottles of house-infused soju (Korean rice wine) used in fusion drinks such as the Sojito (a soju mohito). You will discover an intimate open kitchen that is tiled in blue glass and welcomes conversation between chef and guest. You will see two sides to the menu: Traditional and Modern.

Find out why before how. Many cooks know how to braise meat but they don't know why braising makes tough meat tender. Knowing why makes you more creative and able to use techniques in different situations.

—Chef Park

the rain, the flavors. He remembered the deep-fried rice cake he'd buy with spare change while waiting for the bus. He told himself that a restaurant is not simply about the food. It is about invoking memories and creating new translations of what we taste in life and family.

"I think about my childhood when I cook, and I don't have an Italian grandmother," laughs Chan Owner and

Everything about this picture is very different from the traditional Korean restaurants located to the north and south of Seattle — distinctions that were designed with purpose.

On the Traditional side of the menu, there is the Fried Rice Cake that Chef Park remembers from childhood; lovely little pillows of puffed rice gently dressed with a sweet and spicy sauce. There is Kimchi that is made in-house with local Napa cabbage, radish and daikon. There is the Braised Beef Short Rib with fingerling potato, pearl onion, deep fried rice cake and chili. On the Modern side you will find Bulgogi Beef Sliders with Bulgogi rib-eye beef, cucumber kimchi, scallion, chili mayo and brioche from Grand Central Bakery.

If Chef Park had to name a single signature dish, it would be the Oregon Black Cod, purchased fresh from the market's best fish throwers, poached with soy based broth and chili pepper powder and served with bok choy.

The black cod shares his fresh and local story, the flavor is all about Korea, and the bok choy, traditionally a Chinese vegetable, represents Seattle and its immigrant history.

"I want Americans to know more about Koreans, but I also want them to experience healthy food, smaller portions, heavy with vegetables and local products, which is how Korean peasants traditionally ate," says Park.

This is where Park hopes Korean cuisine is moving in the United States. Although he wouldn't admit it to me, Chef Park, just 30 years old, seems to be working as a leading trendsetter, in Seattle at the very least.

STUFFED YUBA WITH BOK CHOY VEGETABLE BROTH

| 20 | yuba (deep fried tofu skin), sold in any Asian grocery store |
| 20 | long scallions |

FILLINGS

1	lb fresh shrimp, peeled and chopped in small chunks
1	Tbs chopped chive (Chinese chive if possible)
½	cup vermicelli noodle (cooked and chilled), chopped

SAUCE

2	Tbs soy sauce
1	tsp chopped garlic
1	tsp sugar
1	tsp rice vinegar
3	baby bok choy
3	cups vegetable broth or stock
1	dried Thai chile
1	tsp chopped garlic
	Thinly sliced scallions for garnish

• Blanch yubas in boiling water and rinse with cold water until all oil has been washed away. • Cut one end of yuba, split, form a pocket, and squeeze out all the water (If you squeeze without cutting one end, the yuba may explode and become unusable).

• Blanch scallions for 30 seconds or less, cool in ice water, and squeeze out all the water.

• Mix all filling ingredients and sauces and marinate for 10 minutes. • Stuff the fillings into the yuba pocket and tie with scallion, repeat for all yubas. (Can be made ahead and kept in the refrigerator up to 3 days)

• Heat the saucepan and cook garlic for 30 sec (do not burn the garlic). • Add dried chile and bok choy and cook for another 30 seconds.

• Add vegetable broth and stuffed yuba pockets into the sauce pan and gently simmer for 10 minutes until shrimp is cooked. • Season with salt and freshly ground black pepper. • Serve in a bowl with scallions on top.

SEATTLE • PIKE PLACE/POST ALLEY

LA BÊTE

SALT AND PEPPER PORK RINDS

with jalapeño vinegar salt served with pickled shallots. House-made, fried a la minute. Mouths pop. Heads turn. Carnivorous dreams are answered.

We could stop there. But we won't.

La Bête in Capitol Hill is a space filled with thoughtful, beautiful, house-made food that, quite simply, people like to eat.

And La Bête, the place, is as magical as La Bête, the food. Meticulously curated, the brick front suite is filled with old-world charm that mixes cleverly with vintage cool. Filled with huge pieces of modern art and antique details like flickering candles, wood-framed windows and dripping chandeliers, one step inside and you know you've stumbled upon something very special. Many liken the experience to dropping into the rabbit hole in Alice in Wonderland. Bewitching. A game of choices. A duality of natural and artificial.

Aleks Dimitrijevic, chef and owner of La Bête, is the mastermind behind the aesthetic of La Bête. It is not surprising that, on top of being a Culinary Institute of America trained chef, he is also a classically trained artist. The art that fills the walls is his. The Asian-silkscreen-inspired tables that surprise with utterly fascinating details are also his.

His eye for design extends to his plates of food. Chicken Liver Mousse with toasts. Charcuterie Board with house-made pork head cheese and foie gras. The La Bête Deluxe Painted Hills Burger with grilled onion, mushroom, Gruyere cheese and remoulade. House-made Potato Gnocchi with shimegi mushroom sauce, leek, bacon, summer squash, Parmesan speck brodo, and Parmesan cheese.

This clever, beautiful food is a treat for the eyes as much as it is a treat for the taste buds. This is not high-end edible sculpture, mind you, but thoughtfully played colors, textures and placement by someone who understands how light and perspective create something that pops and delights and sparks curiosities.

Half Serbian, half Italian, Aleks has cooked in the United States, Spain and Germany. His childhood was split between Serbia and Croatia with his grandmother, and Michigan with his parents. He grew up with an international host of friends and a family that loved food and wine and long Sunday lunches. He remembers the first time he saw a chicken get its throat cut, in a small village outside Belgrade. "I was enthralled by it running around the yard with its head cut off," laughs Aleks.

His cultural background has led to a melting pot of the very best kind. You will notice Middle Eastern and Indian ingredients dancing with European flavors and preparations. The Grilled Quail is served with cauliflower, almond, couscous and saffron jus. The Fromage de Tête has notes of juniper berries. It's as if you're traveling through a life full of journey and worldly expertise.

And perhaps that is the most tempting piece of the La Bête story—the journey. The journey between artist and chef. The journey between America and Serbia. The journey between natural and artificial. The crux where Aleks's life and creative expression comes together. The rabbit hole where curiosity does not lead to trouble, but rather to a fantastical success.

FROMAGE DE TÊTE (PORK HEAD CHEESE)

(you'll need a mold to set)

1   lb of pork cheeks
1   lb of pork tongues
3-4 smaller pigs ears (optional)
2   qts of brine
½   cup of minced shallot, cooked with a little butter and ½ tsp fresh thyme leaves
    Pepper
1   Tbs parsley
1   Tbs chives
1   sheet of gelatine bloomed in ice water

BRINE

2   quarts filtered water
    Salt, enough until it's about ocean flavor
2   grams Pink Curing Salt

SACHET FOR BRINE AND FOR COOKING LIQUID

Several sprigs of fresh thyme
10   ea crushed black peppercorns
10   ea crushed Juniper Berries
5   ea crushed Allspice
1   tsp fennel seed
2   bay leaves

• Bring water and salt to boil, add sachet and let steep for 10 minutes. • Add pink salt to dissolve and cool in refrigerator.

• Brine pork cheeks, tongues and ears for 24-36 hours.

• Remove pork cheeks, tongues and ears from brine, cover with cold filtered water

until it's about 3-4 inches above meat.
• Make another sachet and add it to the water and meat. • Bring up to a simmer and continue to simmer for 2-3 hours, until cheeks and tongues are tender.
• Remove from the cooking liquid with slotted spoon or spider. • Reduce the cooking liquid by half and reserve warm (adding 1 sheet of bloomed gelatine leaf to the warm liquid to dissolve).

• Peel the membranes from the tongues while still warm. • Finely chop 1/2-3/4 of the pork cheeks, or shred with fingers, leaving the remainder in larger chunks. Julienne the pork ears. In a mixing bowl combine the split tongues, shredded and chunky cheeks and pig ears.

• Add the sweated shallot and most of the cooking liquid to the meat mix, season with black pepper. The mixture should be salty enough from the cooking liquid, but should you like more salt, add it at this point. (Important to add the cooking liquid warm to this mix so that everything is warm before it gets put into the desired mold.)

• Spray desired mold with baking spray and line with plastic wrap. (Bread pan works fine for a mold.) • Put the meat mixture in the mold and lightly press with plastic wrapped cardboard cut to the shape of the top of the mold.
• Refrigerate for 6 hours or overnight.

• Slice to desired portion and plate.

• Garnish with whole grain mustard, cracked pepper, greens, bread and pickled vegetables or cornichons.

What is Head Cheese?

First things first. Head cheese is not cheese. It is a terrine or meat jelly made with meat from the head of a calf or a pig. It is brined, set in a mold with gelatin, and sliced either cold or at room temperature – a preparation that has existed in different forms as peasant food since the Middle Ages. While the thought of acquiring pork cheeks, tongues and ears might seem daunting to you, it's not a difficult order for your butcher.

PINTXO

IN THE HEART OF SEATTLE, A CITY where fresh seafood is as intrinsic to life as the air, you might be surprised to find a small tapas restaurant serving canned imported clams.

These aren't just any canned clams, though—they are Galicia clams and they have a story that could rival even the best fish coming out of Pike Place Market.

For 300 years, fisherwomen called mariscadoras have traveled to Galicia's shores in northwestern Spain to dig for shellfish. Much like clammers on the Puget Sound, these women follow the tides to uncover cockles, razor clams and mussels. Their trade creates an iconic image on the coastline and has also established a luxuriously delicious canned seafood scene in Spain, one that receives high marks from the likes of Anthony Bourdain.

"We've had Spanish women come in and order our Berberechos, which are these absolutely gorgeous marinated clams from Galicia served with bread. It's a unique thing that you can bring to life for these women that have memories of watching mariscadoras swarm the shores," says Amanda Akin, co-owner of Pintxo.

Amanda Akin and Cory Chigbrow opened Pintxo with a simple idea in mind: Create approachable, authentic tapas. The 800-square-foot space they claimed quickly became what they envisioned – a neighborhood spot where Galician clams dance on a menu with fresh, local seafood from the market. Where flavors of San Sebastian, Bilbao and Valladolid waft through a space adorned with art and rustic walls and the best outdoor patio in Belltown. A welcoming space where Spanish guitar filters through the front door.

"Not many people in the city were making tapas approachable. We loved the idea," said Amanda.

The Basque word pintxo (pronounced pin-cho) means "small bite" and even though the cozy space inside also warrants the name, nothing is small about this Belltown hot spot. The Bacon Wrapped Dates stuffed with goat cheese are close to famous, as is the paella that is sometimes made on the sidewalk out front in the summer. You'll find Serrano hams, manchego cheeses, traditional Spanish tortillas, cured

We've always loved the idea of small plate eating. It works especially well at small gatherings in your home or for dinner parties. Tapas are meant to bring people together! Each plate should have unique individual and memorable flavor - they allow people to connect over food and try a variety of different wine/food pairings.

—Amanda Akin, co-owner

meats, imported specialty items, and a cocktail menu that refreshes with house-made Sangria and a brilliant Lavender Pisco Sour made with Alto de Carmen Pisco, lemon, egg white and lavender infused simple syrup.

The menu, the atmosphere and the friendly smiles are indicative of a husband and wife team that are fully devoted to the beauty of their surrounding neighborhood.

"We are totally ingrained in this neighborhood," said Amanda, who lives with husband Cory upstairs from the restaurant. "We live, work, eat and drink within a two-block radius and most of our employees live within ten blocks."

This close relationship with the neighborhood is reminiscent of a small Spanish village, a connection that can be felt through the food and ambiance inside. It has allowed Amanda and Cory to forge partnerships with patrons, and when they were married in 2012, many of their regulars joined them to celebrate.

Pintxo is open seven days a week from 11am-11pm. In addition to lunch and dinner, they serve an outstanding brunch on Saturday and Sunday mornings that includes Dungeness Crab Cakes, a Smoked Salmon Scramble, and a Dulche de Leche French Toast, as well as a selection of tapas.

"Brunch at Pintxo is the city's best kept secret," said Amanda. Which, really, is the best way to describe dining with Amanda and Cory. Whether on the brick-walled patio under the twinkle of globe lights, or indoors at the bar one step inside, one bite of a thoughtfully prepared tapas lined with history and cultural flavor and you'll feel like you've stumbled on the best secret in all of Belltown.

RABO DE TORO (BRAISED OXTAIL)

Rabo de Toro is a long time favorite in Spanish homes around the country. The prize of a bullfighter! We do our best to honor the tradition of Rabo de Toro at Pintxo. We use our favorite Tempranillo wine from the Ribera Del Duero region of Spain, Vega Murillo.

5	lbs oxtail
2	large carrots – cut in quarters
1	large onion – large julienne
2	stalks celery – large chop
1	leek – julienne
16	oz can of chopped tomatoes
3	sprigs fresh thyme
1	bay leaf
4	cloves garlic – crushed
1	tsp black peppercorns
6	cups vegetable stock
1	bottle Vega Murillo Tempranillo red wine
¼	cup Spanish olive oil
	Salt and pepper to taste

• Preheat oven to 350°.

• Create a sachet out of thyme, bay leaf, garlic and peppercorn by placing all items into cheesecloth and securing it with kitchen twine. • Break down the oxtail by cutting through the joints (if you know your butcher, ask them to do it for you).
• Generously salt and pepper the oxtail. • Heat olive oil in a Dutch oven over medium heat. • Brown oxtail on all sides, rendering as much fat as possible. •

Remove oxtail, add onions, celery, carrot, leeks and sachet. • Cook vegetables until tender to the touch. • Deglaze with 2 cups of Vega Murillo Tempranillo Red wine – reduce to half.

• Add oxtail back to the pot. • Add diced tomato, remainder of red wine and veggie stock – enough to just cover the meat and vegetables. Bring to a boil.
• Remove from heat, cover with lid and place into the oven.

• Cook for at least 2 hours, until the meat falls off the bone (checking on the meat after one hour and adding liquid as needed).

• Remove from oven and allow to cool.
• Pull meat from bones, being careful to remove as much meat as possible.

• Remove sachet and discard. Remove the vegetables. Use a sieve to push the liquid into a saucepan. • Boil to reduce the liquid, skimming off all impurities, to a thick consistency. • When the sauce is ready, add the oxtail and simmer until the meat is warmed through. • Serve over a parsnip and potato mash.

MATT'S IN THE MARKET

CHEF SHANE RYAN ALWAYS SAID he'd never live in Las Vegas.

And then along came Joël Robuchon's The Mansion.

In 2005, fresh out of culinary school in Seattle, Shane managed to join the opening crew of The Mansion, now a three Michelin Star restaurant. Under the bright lights of Sin City, he "cut his teeth" under the watchful eye of one of the world's best, Robuchon.

"Yeah, the Vegas thing, it kinda worked out," chuckled Shane.

And it was there, in the center of the country's grandest culinary production, that his quest for adventure really began.

Spurred on by a deep-seated need to learn and cook in other parts of the world, in 2007, Shane hopped on a plane and flew halfway around the world to Bhutan to manage the western and Thai kitchens of a boutique resort in the Himalayas. From Bhutan, he skirted to the Caribbean as head chef of another prestigious establishment in St. Maarten.

For a kid that started out as a dishwasher at the age of 15, his professional life had grown rather stellar. And the tropical destinations that came with his world-tour were an obvious perk. But there was a day when Shane began to miss the personal connection between farmer, chef and diner. He missed the inspiration of lush produce and freshly cured meats. He wished for fresh, local seafood caught the day of service. He wanted access to artisanal products and markets.

It's important to fail in a few recipes here and there and then try again. You may not get it the first time, but pay attention to your mistakes. All of a sudden it will come together and you will have learned something that will translate again and again.

—Shane Ryan, head chef

He needed to go home. To the Pacific Northwest. And so he did. Seattle welcomed him home with open arms and added marks to his resume that were more than impressive. Upon his return, Shane helped to open some of the city's, and arguably, the country's, top restaurants including Tavolata, How To Cook A Wolf, and Staple and Fancy.

But it was his move to Matt's in the Market that is most meaningful to this Seattle chef story. Exceptional product, authentic connections, a vibrant market just steps away, a brilliant team that was "so easy to work with," and proximity to the Olympic Mountains and some of his favorite mushroom foraging spots. Matt's in the Market was his new adventure, all wrapped up in a neat, iconic, homey and utterly irreplaceable package in the heart of Pike Place Market.

"Matt's in the Market's history is flattering and it's so awesome to be able to sustain that. It keeps us on our toes. It

surprisingly easy to talk to and the open format of Matt's kitchen welcomes conversation between chef and guest.

Celebrating community, local sustainability and seasonality, Shane has created an inspired menu highlighting the market fresh ingredients provided by Pacific Northwest farmers, foragers, fisherman and winemakers. Grilled Calamari with peruano beans, Fresno chiles, oregano, pickled sea beans, and tomato-ink sauce. Beef Carpaccio with soft boiled quail egg, Olsen Farms potato chips, and parsley oil. Kurobuta Pork Tenderloin with confit fingerling potatoes, ham hock, pickled beans, and Chicharrón Wild Salmon with fava beans, English peas, mint pesto, marcona almonds, radish, and wild greens.

forces more creativity every year," said Shane.

Despite his decorated and impressive background, diners and coworkers will tell you that Shane is a humble, approachable and fun guy, in and out of the kitchen. He's

"This is an inspirational place to be. We have the country's best market just below us. If you get stuck, all you have to do is take a walk down to the stalls," said Shane.

And that's something you won't find in Vegas.

GRILLED PORK CHOP
With Sweet Corn, Oregano, Rainier Cherries and Ham Hock

(Serves 4)

3	lbs bone-in pork rack
1	lb ham hock cut into 2" pieces
1	lb Rainier cherries
1	bunch fresh oregano
4-6	ears fresh sweet corn
2	sweet onions
	Kosher salt
	Black pepper

• Preheat oven to 350°

• Place the ham hock in a pan and cover the hocks with water. • Cut one onion into chunks and place in the pan with the ham hock and cover with foil.
• Place in the oven for 2 hrs or until tender.

• In the meantime, cut the corn kernels off the cob and set aside. Discard the cobs. • Small dice the other sweet onion and set aside. • Pick the leaves off the stems of the oregano bunch and set the leaves aside. • With a cherry pitter,

pit the Rainier cherries and set aside.

• Fire up the grill. • While waiting for the grill to become hot, pull the rack from the refrigerator and liberally season the pork rack with salt and pepper. Keep at room temperature until ready to grill.

• Arrange and spread the coals on a charcoal grill to one side on medium-high heat. • On a gas grill adjust the temperature to medium high. • Place the pork rack fat cap side down onto the grates. • Turn every 2-3 minutes, twice. • Mark the other side of the pork rack turning every 2-3 minutes twice.
• You can finish cooking the rack on the grill or remove and place the pork into the oven for 20 minutes. • Using a thermometer, pull the pork rack when it has reached a temperature of 140°.
• Cover with foil and let rest.

• Remove the ham hock from the oven. Use tongs to remove from the liquid.

• Pick the meat from the bone. Reserve the liquid.

• In a medium sauté pan on medium heat sauté the sweet onion and corn until tender. • Add the picked ham hock and some of the reserved liquid to make a sauce.

• To plate, spoon the corn and ham hock ragout onto four plates. • Slice the pork rack and place on top of the ragout.
• Garnish with fresh oregano and Rainier cherries. Eat and enjoy!

LLOYDMARTIN

⍳ WHILE STUDYING ENGLISH

Literature and Musical Engineering at Columbia College in Chicago, Sam Crannell realized that his professional dream might not work out the way he had planned.

"I realized I wasn't going to be a writer, and I wasn't going to be a rock star," laughed Sam.

Then one day he cooked a meal for his mother and she said to him, "You should do this."

And so began Sam's foray into the restaurant landscape of Chicago. While still taking classes, he worked in the kitchen of the Chicago Yacht Club, a fascinating pot of

who's who in city life. Sam observed the activity, the volume, the parties, the food, the windy-city celebrities. He loved the sense of chaos and knew he'd thrive in it. So, he dropped out of Columbia College and signed up for a 2-year culinary program.

He finished in 14 months at the top of his class.

Realizing then that cooking was his true calling, Sam began to think about a concept that would come to be years later in a difficult to define section of Seattle. He began to think about the neighborhood restaurant—its meaning, its role, its importance. He launched a career in Seattle that included the favored gastropub kitchens of Quinn's, Oddfellow's and 5 Corner Market Bar & Kitchen.

> *Keep it simple. Less is more. The better the ingredients the better the outcome.*
> —Sam Crannell, executive chef and owner

Then, in 2012, along with his wife Tracey, he opened LloydMartin (named after his two grandfathers) in Queen Anne with a penny-pinching budget and an unapologetically tiny kitchen housing just two plug-in electric cooktops and an oven.

"I used to work for tyrants and brilliantly insane people. Then I decided to become one," said Sam.

It's an interesting thought that certainly pushed forward the entrepreneurial spirit of a chef that tells us he has become known as the "black sheep chef of Seattle." His food, however, on the game- and seasonal-focused

> *"The black sheep chef of Seattle" was named "Best New Restaurant 2012" by Seattle Magazine.*

menu at LloydMartin, can be described more simply and with less drama. His food is all about creating a deeper sense of comfort in a culinary scene that is always trying to go above and beyond the expected; to us, the antithesis of tyrannical and insane, albeit brilliant in its own right.

The menu at LloydMartin is constantly changing, but there are a few dishes that stand out to Crannell as indicative of the restaurant's ongoing inspired spirit. The Rabbit Ravioli with truffled veloute takes a somewhat exotic game and pairs it with pristine truffles. The Pan Seared Scallops with pumpkin risotto and chestnut fondant shows off a tremendous skill and precision without being pretentious. The Foie Gras Mousse is classic and unassuming and perfectly gorgeous. The Elk Bolognese with Huckleberry Sauce is something for the books, if you happen to catch it during huckleberry season.

"We continue to concentrate on making sure that we're not cooking above our diners' heads," said Sam.

In a city where trends in molecular gastronomy and celebrity chefdom dance with old world tradition and immigrant influence, Chef Sam's view is relatively simple. The best ingredients. Honest treatment. Period.

The "Snacks" menu is simple, and again centered on the best ingredients. At $7 a snack, this is a perfect option for quick bites and drinks from their craft cocktail menu. Speaking of cocktails, you will not find Absolut Vodka or Jack Daniel's in the LloydMartin bar. You will find one of the best bartenders in the city, Tyler Kingdom, hand-picking artisan styles of alcohol which are used in creative plays on old classics such as the Gimlet Picasso.

The restaurant is warm and friendly with wood-paneled walls and dim lights. The small staff of eight is passionate and caring and 100 percent committed to the philosophy of soul cooking.

"We've always based everything on knowing that the product we are using is absolutely the best we can find. We feel the same way about the people that work here," said Sam.

LloydMartin was named "Best New Restaurant 2012" by *Seattle Magazine*.

Photos Rachell Taylor

WHITE BEAN MOUSSE ON TARTINE WITH VEGETABLES

(Makes enough for 24 tartines)

WHITE BEAN MOUSSE:

4	cups white beans cooked and still warm
2	Tbs black truffle butter
¼	lb Plugrá butter
	Salt

• Put all into a Cuisinart and puree until smooth and creamy.

TARTINE:

• Slice focaccia bread ¼" thick by 6" long.
• Place on a sheet pan and brush with olive oil. • Sprinkle with sea salt and bake at 350° until crunchy, about 10-15 minutes.

GARNISH:

Really good olive oil
Cornichons halved length-wise
Sliced radish
Marinated olives
Cherry tomatoes
Shaved Parmesan

• You can add any vegetables you like or go crazy and add some bacon or ham!

DIRECTIONS:

• Use a piping bag to place a thick strip of mousse down the center of the bread, then artfully place your garnish.

Shopping Tip

Chef Sam likes to buy his black truffle butter at La Buona Tavola in Pike Place Market. It can be found at most specialty stores or online at Williams-Sonoma.

SEATTLE • QUEEN ANNE

LLOYDMARTIN   1525 QUEEN ANNE AVENUE N • LLOYDMARTINSEATTLE.COM   206.420.7602

71

LECŌSHO

THE SEEDS OF LECŌSHO WERE planted at the opening of another well-known Seattle restaurant, Toulouse Petit, in November of 2009.

Matt Janke (the former and founding chef-owner of Matt's in the Market) and Jill Buchanan, both old friends and colleagues, ran into each other by chance at the premiere party and started talking about how fun it would be to work together again.

The following September, Jill and Matt opened their restaurant, Lecōsho, at The Harbor Steps in downtown

Seattle. With a combined 40+ years of experience in the restaurant industry, you will be hard-pressed to find more experienced and finessed owners than Jill and Matt.

A casually elegant atmosphere, Lecōsho serves quite simply "food we like." Featuring European-influenced dishes using the best ingredients available from the Northwest including herbs, cheeses, wild mushrooms and seafood, plus locally and sustainably farmed pork, lamb, chicken and beef, Lecōsho makes the best of what the season and region offers, on every single plate.

At the pinnacle of this philosophy is the Lecōsho Porchetta. Rated as a Top 10 Dish of 2011 by *Seattle Met*, this pork belly wrapped pork tenderloin, dressed in pork jus, and rested atop a lovely bed of fragrant white bean and baby turnip ragout could easily be the crowned poster child of this restaurant, or Seattle if given a fair chance. It became a signature dish instantly, and can often be found on the lunch

The Lecōsho Porchetta, rated as a Top 10 Dish of 2011 by Seattle Met, *is pork belly wrapped pork tenderloin, dressed in pork jus, and rested atop a lovely bed of fragrant white bean and baby turnip ragout. It could easily be the crowned poster child of this restaurant.*

menu as well, stuffed into a ciabatta roll with arugula and mustard or rendered into the hand-cut tagliatelle carbonara.

As evidenced by the porchetta, as well as the name Lecōsho itself, pork is a big part of the story here. Lecōsho, in Chinook jargon, means "pig." The Lecōsho logo sports a well-fed, well-bred, bucolic pig. Beyond the porchetta, you'll see notes of porky goodness throughout the menu, from what Jill calls "the best pork chop ever" to their elevated version of a BLT to the charcuterie board.

But pork is not all you'll find at Lecōsho. Seafood, chicken, house-made ravioli and game complete the picture and lead each guest into Jill and Matt's personal style of eating and cooking. The Roasted Mad Hatcher Half Chicken is beautifully simple, served alongside Bluebird Farms creamy farro, braised greens and lemon. The Mad Hatcher Rabbit Ragu and Papperdelle is another favorite, where house pancetta makes an appearance with the rabbit as the star. The Grilled Octopus, a small plate, shines with harissa, sautéed fingerling potatoes, asparagus and espelette oil.

Owner operated, Lecōsho's goal is to always be on hand to serve simple, well-prepared food. Chances are good that it will translate to "food *you* like" and beckon a return to the Harbor Steps again and again.

LECŌSHO CHARGRILLED PRAWN
With Chile-Creamed Corn

(Recipe courtesy of Jon Norgren, Lecōsho sous chef)

Oil for cooking
1   Tbs garlic, sliced
1   Tbs shallot, minced
1   Tbs Fresno chiles, diced fine
2   cups sweet corn, grilled and removed from cob
3   Tbs grilled baby onion, chopped
1   cup heavy cream
2   Tbs unsalted butter
    Sea salt, black pepper, red chile flake
8   large prawns, peeled and deveined
    Tomato Oil for garnish (see recipe below)
½   cup shaved fennel (reserve some of the fronds)
    Segments of one orange, juice reserved
    Good quality extra virgin olive oil

• In a sauté pan over medium-high heat, sweat the garlic, shallots and Fresno chiles in oil for approximately 1½ minutes. • Add the grilled corn and onions and sauté for another minute or so, and then add the cream. • Reduce by half, then remove from heat and stir in the butter. • Season to taste with salt, pepper and red chile flake.

• In a small bowl, toss together the shaved fennel and orange segments, including reserved juice. • Add a bit of sea salt and enough extra virgin oil to coat. • Set aside.

• Grill the prawns over hot charcoal.
• Spoon the Fresno chile-corn mixture into a serving bowl, then arrange the prawns around the edge. • Pile the fennel-orange salad in the center.
• Garnish with fennel fronds and Tomato Oil.

TOMATO OIL
1   cup roasted tomatoes
1½   cups good quality olive oil
2   cloves garlic (or roasted garlic)

• Blend all ingredients together, then strain through a fine sieve. • Refrigerate until using.

SERAFINA OSTERIA & ENOTECA

IT HAS BEEN SAID that Serafina echoes the welcoming embrace of an Italian home. Perhaps nowhere is the Serafina embrace felt more authentically today than in the heart of Executive Chef Christian Chandler, who returned to Serafina in the spring of 2013 after a two-year departure, including one year as chef at Lecosho (see page 72).

Now, he feels like he has returned home.

"It is so great to be back here," said Christian. "I love the people. We're a little family here and it shows."

Once Serafina sous chef in his early 20s, he is now head chef in his late 20s, Christian is putting out beautiful, authentic dishes that recreate many of the experiences owner Brooklyn-born Susan Kaufman enjoyed in friends' homes throughout Italy. He is also a member of Kaufman's self-proclaimed "Brat Pack," young men that started their training early under her longtime chefs John Neumark and Dylan Giordan and have now taken over where their mentors left off.

The hallmarks of Christian's kitchen are manifold. Gnocchi di Barbabietole, beautiful little house-made beet gnocchi with sautéed beet greens, fava beans, mint and goat cheese. This may be the most beautiful, colorful and tasteful dish you've ever seen. Polpettini di Vitello, Serafina's famous veal meatballs simmered in green olive-tomato sauce and tossed with penne rigate. Pancia di Maiale, slow-roasted Lan Roc Farms pork belly with juniper-cranberry compote, candied walnuts and chervil. Pappardelle con Salsicce, hand-cut pappardelle with

wild boar sausage, tomato crudo, marjoram and Pecorino Romano.

These are dishes that reflect the landscape of Italy, but also showcase the best of locally sourced, fresh ingredients of the Northwest, something that Christian says is very important to Serafina. From mushrooms to meat, leeks to seafood, he works with as many local producers and purveyors as possible.

Since its opening in 1991, Serafina has become a destination restaurant in the intimate neighborhood along Eastlake between the University and Downtown. Its romantic vibe, felt in the sultry dining room and the vine-laden patio, makes it a haven for couples in love. The live jazz that reverberates through the space only accentuates a dining experience full of passion.

The bar program boasts house-made infusions that utilize the best of Seattle's seasonal fruits and produce. Depending on the time of year, you'll find raspberry vodka, cinnamon tequila, heirloom peach vodka, bitter orange whisky and apple bourbon. We recommend you order an Elisir del Fiore, the most popular and seductive of their house cocktails made with gin, St. Germain elderflower liqueur and lemon juice, shaken into a martini glass and topped with Prosecco and a grapefruit slice.

When you're ready for a bottle of wine, solicit the expert guidance of sommelier Salomon Navarro, who joyfully and passionately tastes hundreds of bottles each month to find the best selections for the restaurant's Wine Club, called "Sal's Picks." Serafina boasts a tremendous wine list that includes fun and different varietals from the Middle East, Greece, Italy and Spain.

Serafina might be the best place on earth to experience the ritual of coming together, over food, over drink, over wine, over conversation and connection. Dining at this Eastlake hot spot is a spirited, beautiful experience, and we agree, reminiscent of the warmest Italian embrace. Go to Serafina, and no matter who you dine with, you will feel loved.

About Rabbit

Rabbit has been used in every region in Italy for hundreds of years and is often found on the dinner table. Lower in cholesterol and fat than other meats, it is flavorful and worth seeking out from your local butcher or market. Food & Wine restaurant editor Kate N. Krader called rabbit "the great new sustainable meat" for 2013 because of the animal's reproductive prowess and whole rabbits are easy to find these days. For this recipe, ask your butcher to grind the hindquarter meat for you and take home some of the carcass to make your own rabbit stock. The rabbit is also delicious braised, fried, stewed or grilled.

POLPETTINE DI CONIGLIO
(Rabbit Meatballs with Tuscan Kale and Pecorino Fresco)

- 5 lbs rabbit hindquarters, deboned and finely ground
- 5 lbs pork butts, finely ground
- 12 whole eggs
- 2 cups finely ground breadcrumbs
- ½ cup grated Parmesan cheese
- ½ cup kosher salt
- 1 Tbs ground allspice
- 1 Tbs ground clove
- 2 Tbs ground juniper
- ½ cup fresh sage, finely chopped
- 1 bunch Tuscan kale, stems removed and chopped
  Grated pecorino fresco
  Chicken stock or rabbit stock

• Combine pork and rabbit along with eggs in large bowl. • In smaller bowl combine breadcrumbs, Parmesan, spices and sage. • Mix well to combine then transfer to rabbit/pork mixture and mix well until combined.

• With 2 oz scoop, portion into balls and refrigerate until ready to cook.

• Heat 1 Tbs of oil in medium sauté pan. • Add 3 meatballs and brown on all sides. • Add kale and ¼ cup chicken stock. Heat 5 more minutes then transfer to earthenware dish. • Cover meatballs with 2 tablespoons of pecorino and place in 425° oven for 8 minutes until golden brown.

HUNGER 2.0

SOMETIMES, THE ROOTS OF A
restaurant sprout in unlikely places—Microsoft, for example.

A cult following, no matter where it's found, can lead a chef, or a pair of chefs, to birth something beautiful.

"We were executive chefs for this *local conglomerate*," quipped Brian Brooks, chef and co-owner of Hunger 2.0. "One day one of our fans said, 'Why don't you start your own restaurant?'"

"Indeed," said Brian and wife, chef and co-owner Jaime Mullins. "Why not?"

They found a tiny, 30-ft space on upper Fremont to house their joint project, a concept called Hunger. Jaime grouted the floors. Brian built the bar. They cooked on camp stoves. Brian held tight to his desire to do something cool and unique. Jaime became known for her paella that drew from her background in Spanish cuisine.

And *hunger* drove them both. Hunger for a challenge. Hunger to do something great. Hunger to have fun.

And with a new cult following, this time from Fremonsters passionate about supporting a neighborhood business and also harboring an addiction to the Hunger brunch's most popular act—The Chicken and The Egg (a boneless piece of buttermilk fried chicken and a poached egg topped with hollandaise, served over sautéed kale), Hunger was creating in their guests exactly what its name suggested.

In love with the neighborhood, Brian and Jaime decided to expand to a larger location in the heart of Fremont. They called it Hunger 2.0 and opened in May 2012, just short of two years since Hunger's smaller premiere.

"It was like, wow! A real hood! An outdoor patio! The creature comforts of a bigger kitchen and space were amazing to us," said Brian.

Today, the space seats 80 inside and an additional 30 out on the patio, providing welcomed elbow room for their guests old and new. And a larger kitchen? It's the bee's knees for the Hunger 2.0 team

in so many ways, but most exciting has been their newly realized focus on in-house butchery, charcuterie and meat grinding.

Hunger 2.0 regularly turns out fun, inspired food that is committed to local sources and preparations. They cure their own salmon. The ricotta is house-made. The nuts are roasted and seasoned with a homemade mix. The chorizo is house-made.

The house-made meats come together beautifully in dishes like the Chorizo Stuffed Dates, where Brian and Jaime are able to take something expected and make it unique. The dates are stuffed with house-made chorizo and bacon and served with Valdeon ice cream. It's finished off with a balsamic reduction and smoked paprika oil.

The brunch is still phenomenal and always worth a trip to Fremont. Also uniquely Hunger 2.0, the "Hangover Hour" runs every Saturday and Sunday 1-2pm with special rates on Mimosas, Bloody Marys and, of course, The Hangover Breakfast—Moroccan spiced hand-cut fries, sunny up eggs, disco gravy and smoked cheese sauce. (If that doesn't fix you up, nothing will!)

Always inventive. Always fresh. Always fun.

"We really wanted to help Fremont become what it should be," said Brian.

With its focus on continental and Mediterranean cuisine, Hunger 2.0 is just what Fremont's free-spirited, playful, center-of-the-universe collective needed.

Quick Tip

Start with the best ingredients you can find and take the time to follow the instructions. If you do this, you will end up with an amazing dish every time.

—Brian Brooks, chef and co-owner

PAELLA

RISOTTO BASE (3 CUPS)

- 2 Tbs unsalted butter
- ½ cup onions, diced ¼"
- 2 cups Arborio rice
- 4 cups chicken broth

• In a round braising pan, melt butter. Add onions and sauté, stirring constantly until translucent. • Add Arborio rice and sauté, stirring constantly until slightly translucent. DO NOT BROWN! • Add chicken broth, one cup at a time, and simmer, stirring constantly, until no liquid releases when you pull it away from the bottom with a spoon. • Spread on a sheet pan and refrigerate until cold.

PAELLA BROTH (4 CUPS)

- 4 cups chicken stock
- 1 Tbs lobster base
- 1 tsp saffron threads
- 1 tsp chile flakes
- ½ tsp turmeric
- 1 Tbs garlic, minced

• Mix ingredients together until lobster base is fully dissolved. • Place in a large

container and refrigerate until needed. Be sure to stir again before use.

TOMATO BUTTER

- 1 oz wt. unsalted butter
- ¼ tsp fresh thyme, minced
- ½ tsp fresh Italian parsley, minced
- ½ tsp tomato paste

• Place all ingredients in a food processor and blend until smooth and well combined. Butter may separate. Keep processing until it comes back together.

PAELLA PRESENTATION

- 1 Tbs olive oil
- 2 oz Chorizo links, cut into 1-inch chunks
- 2 oz chicken thighs, boneless, skinless, cut into 1-inch chunks
- 3 ea clams
- 3 ea mussels
- 3 ea shrimp 16/20
- 1 oz red onion, julienne ¼"
- 1 oz carrots, diced ¼"

- 1 oz roasted red pepper, julienne ¼"
- 3 cups Risotto Base
- 2-3 cups Paella Broth
- 1 oz peas
- 1 batch Tomato Butter
- 6 ea asparagus spears, 4" lengths
- 1 Tbs diced Roma tomatoes
  White wine

• Place paella pan on stove, sauté in pan chorizo and chicken until cooked. • Add onion, carrot, pepper and peas. Cook until onion is translucent. • Deglaze pan with white wine and add risotto.

• Arrange protein in pan pulling shellfish to the top and equally distributed in the pan. Let pan sit on medium heat for five minutes for risotto to settle and crisp up. • Stir in Tomato Butter. • Arrange asparagus and finish by placing in a 450° oven for 5-7 minutes to lightly brown the dish and dry up excess liquid.

• Garnish with Roma tomatoes and place on a large round plate for service.

MANHATTAN

WHEN YOU'RE TALKING ABOUT Manhattan, the restaurant, it's natural to also chat about their Manhattan, the drink.

The recipe? John Jacob rye whiskey, Punt e Mes vermouth, orange bitters and an orange twist. This cocktail is classic, but somehow better and surprising with dark notes of vanilla, slightly sweet caramel and spice.

The same can be said of the food at Manhattan. It is comfort food at its heart, but elevated and surprising in the best of ways.

"We are all about southern style comfort food that's inspired with a modern twist," said Chef Khampaeng Panyathong.

Manhattan's Buttermilk Fried Chicken is an interesting representation of this story line. A crispy fried 'airline' chicken breast is served over white cheddar grits, grilled okra, red pimento peppers and red eye gravy. An airline cut of chicken means that the first winglet is still attached to the breast, giving more tender juiciness to the breast and a piece of meat that appears ready for flight. Frying the breast is not traditional southern style, but with the addition of the winglet it becomes something new and clever, yet recognizable.

This is the key at Manhattan and you can see it all over their menu. The Surf & Turf comes in four versions: Traditional with a 5 oz. filet mignon and 5 oz. lobster tail, but also Steak And Scallops, The Steak Oscar (with crab cakes and hollandaise sauce) and Southern Style (with shrimp in a Cajun cream sauce, white cheddar grits and collard greens).

"American food is where it's at," said Khampaeng.

Khampaeng (pronounced like "campaign" or KP if you must) was born in Laos and raised for a short time in Thailand before moving to Seattle at 2-years-old. He grew up the son of immigrants, eating a very basic Thai diet of steamed vegetables, broiled meat, and spice, with rice as the vehicle. The fact that he is now cooking gently reinvented, indulgent American comfort classics can be traced back to his first cafeteria food experience in the U.S.

"When I first went to elementary school, I always loved cafeteria food. I remember there were two lines, one for burgers and fries and one for the more creative plate. I always went for the burger and fry line," laughed Khampaeng.

He remembers listening to Americans complain about cafeteria food and he didn't understand it. It was always so flavorful and delicious to Khampaeng, the kind of food he wanted to eat all the time. This is how he knew he was in love with American food.

You can see this inspiration in Manhattan's Mac and Cheese that adds the upscale component of pork belly. The Steak Sandwich, a meal any American recalls, is built with New York steak, arugula, blue cheese, caramelized onions, and roasted garlic and horseradish spread. Even the Baked Quinoa Casserole has a certain cafeteria-bred, American home-cooking ring to it, but dig deeper and you'll find a mix of modern and rustic ingredients like quinoa, spinach, corn, tomato, kalamata olives, caramelized onions, white cheddar and brussels sprouts.

Khampaeng believes that American comfort food does not always equate to Southern, and Manhattan pulls from any region where country cooking tells a story.

"Comfort food from any part of the fifty states, we'll do it," said Khampaeng.

So when you dine at Manhattan, arrive a little early. Order the signature Manhattan and the Steak Bites, made with grass-fed beef tenderloin bites, kale, garlic-ginger soy sauce and a side of toasted focaccia. It's a classically elevated beginning to a dinner full of American comfort.

SHRIMP AND GRITS

(Serves 4)

WHITE CHEDDAR GRITS

- 3 cups water
- 1 Tbs salt
- 1 tsp black pepper
- 1 tsp sugar
- 1 whole lemon (juice only)
- 1 cup grits (quick cook grits)
- 1 cup heavy cream
- 2 cups white cheddar (shredded)

• In a medium pot, add water, salt, pepper, sugar, lemon juice, and bring to a boil. • Once the water is at a boil, stir in grits and reduce heat to low. • Continue to cook and stir for about 20 minutes (careful not to let the bottom of the pan burn). • Now add the cream and white cheddar and stir. • Cook for another 10 minutes or until grits are fluffy and cheesy.

SHRIMP IN A CAJUN CREAM SAUCE

- 1 stick butter
- 1 garlic clove, minced
- ¼ cup diced onion
- ¼ cup flour

- 2 cups heavy cream
- 2 cups vegetable broth or shrimp broth or water
- 1 whole lemon (juice only)
- 1 Tbs salt
- 1 tsp black pepper
- 1 tsp cajun seasoning
- 1 tsp sugar
- 1 lb raw shrimp (peeled and de-veined)

• In a large pot, melt butter on medium heat then add minced garlic and diced onion. • Continue to cook onion/garlic for about 3 minutes or until soft. • Now add flour and stir for about 3 minutes or until flour is fully incorporated. • Add cream and broth and stir with a whisk until sauce begins to thicken. • Now add all of the remaining ingredients and simmer for about 5 minutes until the shrimp is cooked.

• Serve shrimp and Cajun cream sauce over grits. Shown below with a piece of pork belly on top.

DELICATUS

🍴 JUST ABOUT FOUR BLOCKS FROM
the roar of CenturyLink Field where Seahawks fans
break sound records, a delicatessen is breaking the mold of
what defines authentic deli in Seattle.

Turning out 300 sandwiches every day, Delicatus is
not your average ham, salami and capacola type of shop,
although you'll find that here too.

What fills the cult-followed lunch menu is a
combination of classic and inventive, east coast and west
coast, traditional and progressive. The space is filled with
flavors and aromas and inspirations that borrow from
authentic European delicatessen history and add in just the
right touch of
authentic Seattle.

Derek
Shankland and
Mike Klotz
opened Delicatus
in Pioneer Square
in March 2010 on
the simple concept
that people in the
greater Seattle area
deserved a better
sandwich.

"You don't
have to sacrifice
fresh, local quality
in a sandwich.
And you shouldn't
have to pay twenty
bucks for it," said
Mike, Delicatus
co-owner.

Katie Lybeck

You'll find two tracks on their lunch menu:
Traditionalists and Progressives. The Pavo Diablo, a top-
selling Progressive, is layered with hickory smoked turkey,
sliced avocado, spinach, cilantro, Havarti, spicy chipotle
aioli, and roasted poblano peppers on sourdough bread. The
classic Reuben, an obvious favorite on the Traditionalist
side, is mounded with flavorful corned beef, house-made
sauerkraut, Swiss Emmental, and spicy Russian dressing on
toasted caraway rye.

The ingredients are as fresh and local as you can get.
The salmon is cured in-house for the Ballard Lox. The
pastrami and corned beef is made in-house as well. And the
list of artisanal purveyors is long and lush, including some
of Seattle's best. Delicatus sandwiches make friends with
Panzanella Bread Company, Frank's Produce, Bavarian Meat,
Olympic Provisions, Mt. Townsend Creamery and many
more.

But Delicatus doesn't close after lunch and Chef Aaron
Willis is making sure Seattle knows it.

Filet Mignon with creamed local mushrooms.
Deconstructed Chicken Pot Pie, an inside-out puff pastry
shell filled with
rotating market
vegetables and
rosemary veloute.
Italian Porcetta
that Mike calls
"the best of all
worlds in one
piece of heavenly
pork." A play on
Duck L'Orange
that dances with
pomegranate
molasses and
pink peppercorn
beurre blanc. A
nod to deli, dinner
at Delicatus is
elevated in the best
of ways.

"We wanted
to do something
more for folks in the neighborhood, to offer an upscale,
Northwest take on cuisine," said Aaron.

With a commissary kitchen just down the block that's
dedicated to pickles, wine, events and a future retail business
that will make Delicatus' homemade dressings, pastrami and
corned beef available to their sandwich-crazed fans, you've
got to wonder what's next for this powerhouse team of deli
denizens.

Michael Henry

WHOLE GRILLED TENDERLOIN

NW Natural beef, whole tenderloin
Delicatus House Steak Seasoning (or
    your favorite mix)
Oil

• Generously coat meat with seasoning. Dress with a little oil and drop on a hot, clean grill. Chef Willis likes to grill the tenderloin whole because it locks in flavor and makes grilling life easy. • Turn "the brick" on all four sides until well-marked, about 3-4 minutes on each side. • Pop the steak into a 500-degree oven for five minutes, or longer, depending on desired doneness. • Pull out when finished and let it rest. Don't disturb it. • After three minutes, put some tented foil over the meat and wait some more. • When it's ready to be sliced to desired thickness, season with sea salt and cracked pepper and top with fixings.

CREAMED MUSHROOM MIX

A simple side dish that can be used with lots of different applications. Delicatus uses a blend of crimini and portabella mushrooms from Olympia, but it is also superb with foraged morel mushrooms should you be so lucky.

For every 1 cup of sliced mushroom, use 1/4 cup cream.

• Sauté mushrooms with a little butter or oil until liquid is absorbed and mushrooms are wilted. • Add cream to the hot pan and turn down to medium high. • Add roasted garlic and reduce cream by half. • Pull mix off heat and add a pinch of grated parmesan cheese and salt/pepper blend. Careful not to over reduce, you want some of that creamy goodness for the steak.

SAUTÉED GREENS

About 2 cups baby or chopped spinach, loosely packed
Clarified butter or oil

• Into a hot pan, drop the greens on top and immediately start moving them around in the pan. • Turn off the heat and toss in a pinch of fresh garlic. • Toss leaves in pan and turn heat back on to medium-high. • Work the greens in the pan until wilted, finish with salt and white pepper to taste.

CRISPY POTATO SKINS

We use Yukon Gold potatoes for this, you want a thin skinned variety for this garnish. These skins for us are a byproduct of the potatoes we use in our chowder and potato salad. It takes one potato to produce enough Crisps for one order.

• Rinse and scrub potato well. • Simply peel the potato from end to end, trying to maintain long smooth strokes and produce long skins.

• Pat skins dry and then fry in 400 degree oil until they crisp up and float to the top of the oil. • Drain on paper towel and lightly season with salt.

Bringing Steak Dinner to the Deli

In honor of the steakhouse experience, Delicatus creates a steak dish during their dinner service that reflects the essence of a classic steakhouse experience, but with a few twists. All the gluttony of a high-end steakhouse at half the price.

SEATTLE · PIONEER SQUARE

LOWELL'S

M MARK MONROE, OPERATOR OF
the iconic Lowell's Restaurant & Bar in the heart of Pike Place Market, is reminded everyday of the history his restaurant inhabits.

Whether it's Mario Batali coming in for his favorite Dungeness Crab Omelet, an elderly man that cooked for Lowell's in its opening year of 1957 showing off the place to his grandchildren, a table filled with three generations of Seattle natives, or a woman feeding her 4 year-old daughter the famous blueberry pancakes she enjoyed as a child, Lowell's holds a place in this city, in this market, that touches people from all ages and stages on a very personal note.

"We were here before the Space Needle," said Mark.

Truth is, Lowell's opened before many of the well-known landmarks in Seattle. With roots that date back to 1906, the original tenant, the flagship "Mannings Cafeteria," roasted coffee and peanuts and served cafeteria fare to the people that visited and worked the Public Market—carriage drivers, fishermen and farmers.

"And it still looks the same from the front—it's one of those intangibles in the city of Seattle, a gift in a time where time moves so fast," said Mark.

And time does move fast. With food celebrities and press putting consistent stamps of approval on this hometown favorite, Lowell's is *the* spot for tourists visiting the market. It's also favored among locals that come for the food and the views and the nooks and crannies that offer prime people watching and a casual atmosphere that

always promises good eats. Today, the 150-seat restaurant covers three floors and offers five different versions of Eggs Benedict during their gigantic breakfast service, on top of a full, fresh philosophy on lunch and dinner. They serve an estimated 800-1000 guests per day during the height of summer.

Despite its volume and size, Lowell's has kept its devotion to high-quality food and ingredients. The salmon is cured in-house to make a lox that will rival any bagel plate you've ever experienced. The meats are slow braised with love, just as they always have been, before being layered inside lunch favorites such as the Smoked & Slow Braised Brisket Sandwich. The kitchen crew traverses the market every day to meet with their favorite purveyors, often making new friends and discoveries.

Mario Batali calls Lowell's his 'Breakfast Roost' when in Seattle, and he always has the Dungeness Omelet!
—**Mark Monroe, Operator**

Authentic old Seattle. Contemporary food that's not trendy. All-American and Pacific Northwest fresh. A family of staff that loves what they do and loves working together. Views of the Puget Sound that continue to blow away locals that return time and time again.

You'll find all of this and more at Lowell's, a place that is lovingly referred to as "the living room" of Pike Place Market.

PACIFIC NORTHWEST DUNGENESS CRAB EGGS BENEDICT

First off, don't be intimidated by the poaching of eggs or the proper whisking up of Hollandaise sauce; neither are magic. You can even take shortcuts that are referenced all over the Internet, just don't skip quality and freshness of ingredients!

2 farm fresh chicken eggs per person
Rustic rosemary bread
Dungeness crab
A classic "Hollandaise Sauce" recipe*

• Toast a couple half slices of rustic rosemary bread, then butter them and throw buttered side down on a medium hot grill. • While doing this, have a pot of simmering water ready that you've thrown a small capful of white vinegar into (this will keep the egg whites together while poaching instead of spreading all throughout the water).

• Crack each egg gently into the simmering water, separate from each other by an inch so as not to poach into each other. Poach for two and a half minutes for runny centers and firm whites.

• Place the two toast halves on a plate, top each with 1½ oz of Dungeness crab, then the poached eggs, and then drape the eggs with the rich, creamy Hollandaise sauce. • Sprinkle a small touch of cayenne over the top for contrast.

• At Lowell's we accompany all of our Benedicts with crispy hash browns, which taste great with the Hollandaise sauce pooling around the plate.

*Hollandaise sauces are all pretty much the same – whipped up with egg yolks, lemon juice, cayenne, salt and unsalted butter – it's the quality of the freshest ingredients that make the difference.

Photos Geoffrey Smith

Your Market Shopping List

Inside Lowell's recipe for the famous Northwest Dungeness Crab Eggs Benedict, you'll find nods to some of their favorite Pike Place Market vendors. We want to give you the inside scoop on each one, so that the next time you're in Seattle or at the market, you'll know who to visit to recreate the dish in true market fashion.

Nancy's Creamery, also known as Pike Place Creamery, for farm-fresh eggs. You know you're getting farm-fresh, straight-from-the-hen eggs when you buy from Nancy. You can also find goose eggs, duck eggs, ostrich eggs and enough milk, butter, ice cream and cow kitsch to "shake a stick at." The creamery is located just across the cobblestones from Lowell's. *1514 Pike Place, Suite 3*

Three Girls Bakery for rustic rosemary bread. Founded in 1912 by, you guessed it, three girls! The bakery is the oldest continually operating business at the Pike Place Market, and the first business in Seattle started by women, with the exception of some houses of ill repute, so they say. Just 10 steps away from the Creamery! *1514 Pike Place, Suite 1*

Pure Food Fish Market for Dungeness crab. This was the first fish vendor in the market. Opened in 1911, it has been family-owned for four generations and still operates as a single long counter in the heart of the market. Speaking of walls, they have a "Dungeness Crab Wall." Really! It's a thing of absolute beauty. If you're visiting from out of town, they'll pack your fish to last 48 hours or ship it anywhere in the U.S. overnight. This key ingredient is not one you want to skimp on. Ask for "Harry," he's been there for 40 years, everyday. He's the guy with the huge black mustache. *1511 Pike Place*

SEATTLE • PIKE PLACE/POST ALLEY

BITTERROOT

Photos Chris Jordan/Shipwreck Design

🍴 BITTERROOT IS NOT your average BBQ joint. No, this is Northwest BBQ in the middle of Ballard.

Sound awesomely unique and utterly intriguing to you? We think so, too. Bitterroot is the BBQ restaurant you never knew you craved, in a place you never knew could plate up classics like ribs, brisket, apple wood smoked chicken, pulled pork, and new twists like smoked pork shank and Buffalo fried chicken livers.

Bitterroot is the dream child of the husband and wife team Hannah Jo and Grant Carter. Hannah Jo manages the front of the house, while Grant is happiest smokin' meat as the chef.

Speaking of meat, Bitterroot's process is a bit different than what most BBQ-loving folks recognize. The meat is dry-rubbed and then smoked dry, meaning it hits the table without a lick of sauce. Hannah Jo says the meat should be tender and juicy from within, not because it's been slathered with a bunch of sauce that's been baked into the meat. The low, slow dry rub method of smoking meat coupled with

the light sweet smoke of Washington applewood creates a uniquely regional flavor and style, a point that was important to the Carters when designing their concept.

"We certainly don't have a map of Texas on the wall," said Grant.

There is sauce, of course, but Bitterroot guests slather it on themselves, at the table. Four house-made versions sit ready for ribs and chicken: Sweet (with flavors of apple and Coca-Cola), Carolina Mustard (sweet and tangy, the Carters' favorite), Spicy (with flavors of chipotle and jalapeños) and Vinegar (hot pepper and garlic vinegar).

But back to that meat. The brisket is one of Bitterroots' signatures.

> *We certainly don't have a map of Texas on the wall.*
> **Grant Carter, chef and co-owner**

The meat is rubbed with a salt and pepper mixture and then smoked for 16-18 hours. Grant leaves more of the fat cap on than traditional brisket in, say, Texas. The Bone-In Pork Belly sits in brine for two days and then hangs out in the smoker for 8-12 hours. The Hot Links are ground and cased in-house. Pretzel buns arrive warm every morning from Tall Grass Bakery, destined for pulled pork, pulled chicken, braised beef and burger sandwiches.

Above and beyond the BBQ and good eats, Hannah Jo and Grant wanted to create a place that had an approachable price point, casual service and an atmosphere that attracted regulars.

"If we were going to be here night and day, we wanted it to represent what we love to eat and drink," said Hannah Jo.

Speaking of drink, you cannot talk about Bitterroot without talking about bourbon. American and rye whiskeys pack the house with 2 oz. pours from more than 100 varieties. The Ballardmaker is a popular way to taste from Bitterroots' collection. The bartender selects a 1 oz whiskey pour plus a half pint draft beer, and it's different every time you order. You can also do a Whiskey Flight for a more robust tasting.

BBQ, bourbon and a whole lot of Northwest Ballard style will meet you inside of Bitterroot. Grab a table in their rustic yet urban dining room or pull up a chair to their bar, a stylish re-cast of a classic saloon with modern lines and cork walls. Stay awhile. And then come back. You're bound to be a newly won fan of Northwest BBQ and the latest edition to the list of Bitterroot regulars.

Takin' Temp

When you're braising meats at a low, slow temperature, don't rely on a thermometer. Rely on how it feels. If there's no tension, then it's most likely done. If it pushes back, then you need to let it keep going.

—Grant Carter, chef and owner

BITTERROOT'S BLOODY MARY

1 can (46 oz) tomato juice
1 qt smoked tomato* puree

*Smoke whole peeled tomatoes for 4 hours at 200º, remove and puree in a food processor.

2½ tsp thyme
2½ tsp garlic powder
2½ tsp paprika
2½ tsp celery salt
2½ tsp black pepper
2½ tsp horseradish
2½ tsp sugar
2 oz Tabasco
2½ oz Worcestershire sauce
2½ oz lime juice
1 oz stout beer
1 oz red wine
½ L vodka, tequila, mezcal, or bourbon!

• Mix all in a large pitcher and serve in pint glass over ice with a smoked salt rim. • Add house-made pickles and maple molasses bacon jerky.

BRINE FOR HOMEMADE PICKLED VEGETABLES

3 cups rice vinegar
1 cup water
½ cup kosher salt
½ cup sugar
2 Tbs whole peppercorn
2 Tbs whole coriander
2 Tbs mustard seed
2 Tbs fennel seed
2 tsp chile flakes

• Bring all ingredients to a boil. Let boil for ten minutes. • Pour hot liquid over vegetables and chill.

• Let it sit for two days and then enjoy. Some of Bitterroot's favorite pickled vegetables and fruit are cauliflower, carrot, asparagus, beet, okra, and apple.

MOLASSES JERKY

2 parts molasses
1 part maple syrup
Bacon

• Mix molasses and syrup. • Submerge bacon pieces into mixture. • Pull out of mixture and wipe excess off of bacon. • Put on trays and dehydrate at 145º for approximately 12 hours or until desired texture.

ROW HOUSE CAFE

🍴 MADE-FROM-SCRATCH comfort. We dare you to find a friend who'll turn that down.

Throw in some wood-worn European charm, a little old world Seattle, a porch that beckons visitors, a breakfast, brunch, lunch and dinner service that's full of flavors and memories, all delicately placed in a pocket of a neighborhood that caters to big-scale industry, and chances are, you and that friend are heading straight for the Row House Café in South Lake Union.

"It's a little slice of Europe in a landscape of glass and steel," said Erin Maher, Row House Café owner.

And that it is. Housed in a row of buildings that date back to shipbuilders' quarters in 1904, the Row House is a nod to a time long gone. Sitting in the center of the Amazon campus behemoth, this bistro and the walls it inhabits is a reminder of what this neighborhood used to be, and thanks to Maher, guests and passers-by will have that reminder for years to come.

"These buildings are one of the last relics in a neighborhood that is under gentrification," said Maher.

Inside, the original woodwork and construction is much the same as it was in 1904. The "completely sustainable" remodel bears hardly anything new, taking advantage of repurposed materials and hand-hewn lumber from the boat docks to repair trim work.

There is no doubt that when you walk in Row House you feel the history and respect the thoughtful approach to keeping it authentic in the middle of a neighborhood that moves so fast.

But it is in the kitchen of Chef Cynthia Rosen where the real made-from-scratch magic happens. It is where she turns out homemade cakes that sell out before they have a chance to find home in the pastry case. It is where she

lovingly makes her Grits and Grillades, a brunch favorite and nod to a past that is cross-cultural, well-traveled, and soul-stirred.

"When you come in here, if you've had an awful day, you can put it behind you," said Cynthia.

Self-taught in the kitchen, Cynthia's culinary career began in Amsterdam. Recently graduated from UC-Santa Barbara with a history degree and not a clue what to do with it, she took off for Europe. She needed a job on her travels and was given the choice between chambermaid or restaurant work. She chose the latter and on a whim was hired as a dishwasher.

"One night the prep cook didn't show up. The owner gave me a knife and showed me how to break down vegetables and that was it," laughed Cynthia.

She continued to travel. She got married. She opened a vegetarian restaurant in Tel Aviv, Israel before making her way back to the States, to her home in Birmingham, Alabama, and then, Seattle.

Her cultural mix of life experiences defines her made-from-scratch magic in many ways. There are pieces of her travels, as well as owner Erin's, through Europe and the Middle East and the south that grace every bite of food.

And if you've convinced that friend to join you for a coffee, a cocktail, breakfast, brunch, lunch or dinner at the Row House—all you can do is hope that you arrive in time to scoop up at least one slice of Chef Cynthia's homemade cake before it disappears for the day.

Photos Eric Over

GRITS & GRILLADES

(Serves 8-10)

ROAST MEDALLIONS

3-4 lb roast
Sea salt and freshly ground pepper
All purpose flour
Canola oil, for frying

GRILLADES

• Slice roast into medallions. • Salt and pepper medallions, tossing in a bowl to coat well. • Let the medallions rest while preparing sauce. • Flour medallions and fry in canola oil. There should be a good inch or so of oil in the pan. Brown both sides. • Add browned medallions to sauce and simmer for about an hour.

GRILLADES SAUCE

½ cup olive oil
1½ cups diced onion
1½ cups diced celery
1½ cups diced green bell pepper
1 cup sliced scallions
¼ cup minced garlic
1½ cups sliced mushrooms
10 tomatoes (whole, canned) shredded
3 Tbs beef base

8 cups water
¼ cup chopped parsley
1 Tbs hot sauce
3 Tbs minced thyme
2 Tbs Worcestershire
Sea salt and freshly ground black pepper

• Sweat vegetables in olive oil. • Add remaining ingredients and simmer.

CREAMY CHEESE GRITS

4 cups grits
16 cups water
¼ lb butter
2 cups shredded sharp white cheddar
2 cups shredded yellow cheddar

• Boil grits, water and butter stirring almost constantly with a whisk. • When it reaches a thick, creamy consistency, add cheeses a little at a time stirring each addition in before adding more. • Salt and pepper.

PLATING

• Dress ½ of the plate with cheesy grits and spoon grillades over the rest of the plate letting them spill onto grits.

ANNAPURNA CAFE

Jason Staats

is massive at first glance, but if you read it slowly, you will see an exuberant exploration of Nepal, India and Tibet. At lunch you'll find a wide array of plates, breads, Thalis, curries, noodle soups, and combination platters that appeal to everyone in search of flavor, including vegetarian, vegan and gluten-free diners.

At dinner, the Tandoori clay oven makes its appearance with Tandoori Chicken, Chicken Tikki, Tandoori Mixed Platter, Tandoori Shrimp and Lamb Boti. In addition, the chicken, lamb, seafood and vegetarian dishes expand and include favorites such as Goat Curry and the Himalayan Curry where Roshita asks you to "dine like a Sherpa and then take a hike." It is the Sherpa's favorite curry sauce, cooked with tomatoes, onions, sweet peas, potatoes, Tibetan herbs and a hint of Szechwan pepper. The Goa Curry, a coconut base curry sauce simmered with fresh curry leaves, onions and cilantro is also a favorite.

WHEN FOOD TRAVELS THROUGH

the world, across borders and over mountains, it evolves in magical ways. This is an idea that has followed Roshita Shrestha, chef-owner at Annapurna Café, around the globe.

Roshita came to Seattle by way of Japan, after many years of experience cooking the foods of her native Nepal, including Newari cuisine. She spent several more years traveling and learning the foods of India and Tibet where she found herself thinking about that moment high in the Himalayas where Nepal meets Tibet. What happens to the food?

"When food travels, it will add some new things. Tibetan is mostly Chinese. Nepalese food uses spices from India. This is a very interesting idea to me," said Roshita.

We always have time for people. If you are too busy for this, you are missing out.

—Roshita Shrestha, chef-owner

This is a concept that is explored in fantastic ways at Annapurna Café, which received the *Seattle Magazine* award for Best Restaurant 2012 in the Indian category. The menu

Located underground, in a nondescript building on Broadway, a walk down the stairs to Annapurna transports you to a cozy atmosphere where dark red and saffron walls meet hanging bells, candles and mandala artwork. Roshita herself, who is always happy

to meet her guests and ensure that they have the best experience at Annapurna, no matter how busy she is, will most likely welcome you.

"We always have time for people. If you are too busy for this, you are missing out," said Roshita.

This is perhaps the most delicious element of Annapurna. The ambiance, the warmth, and the welcoming spirit will bring you back to Roshita's doorway on Broadway. The curry, the naan, the noodles, the tandoori? Exceptional extras.

Jason Staats

GOAT CURRY

¼   cup vegetable oil

2   lbs cubed goat with bone on

¼   cup of garlic and ginger paste mixture

2   Tbs gram masala

3-5   bay leaves

½   Tbs turmeric powder

2   Tbs curry powder

2   onions, chopped

1-2   cups of water

2   bunches of cilantro, chopped

Salt and red chile powder (as needed)

• Heat the oil in large pot. Add chopped onions and cook over low heat until they become soft light brown in color.
• Add turmeric powder, curry powder, garlic and ginger paste and stir over low heat. • Add cubed goat meat and immediately after, add bay leaves, salt and gram masala. • Stir until all the spices and paste are evenly distributed throughout the meat.

• Add one cup of water and stir. • Add more water, up to an additional cup, depending on how much gravy you like. *Annapurna likes to serves thick gravy, cooked with less water.*

• Continue to cook, covered, over low heat for about 45-60 minutes.

• Add salt and chile powder to taste.

• When the gravy is thick at the bottom of the pan and the meat is dark, you are just about done. • At this point, add cilantro, stir and cover. • Turn off the heat and let it sit until you get the first aroma of cilantro.

OSTERIA LA SPIGA

WHEN CHEF SABRINA TINSLEY

came home at the end of a 92-hour workweek, she was met by a spritely young girl ready to follow in her mother's footsteps, just as soon as she is old enough for a work permit.

"My daughter said to me, 'Mom, I can't wait until I'm 15 and can help you in the kitchen.' It's amazing really. She wants to be our pastry chef. Both Pietro and I are eager to teach our kids about this business," said Sabrina.

Enter Osteria La Spiga. An authentic Italian experience of the Romagna region in the heart of Capitol Hill, complete with culinary dedication and passion that spans generations. At the helm is Sabrina, an award-winning chef, public figure, and one of only three Seattle chefs invited on *Food Network's* "Iron Chef America," (where she competed against Bobby Flay, no less.)

As a young girl in Alaska, Sabrina recalls helping her own mother with food duties that today would fall under farm-to-table classification. Giant zucchinis, cabbages

Chef Sabrina Tinsley is one of only three Seattle chefs invited on Food Network's "Iron Chef America" where she competed against Bobby Flay.

and potatoes were the early fruits of Sabrina's labor and experiences that showed her the value of both the earth and hard work.

But it wasn't until she moved out and on to college that she realized she wanted to cook.

The new-found talent brought her to France and eventually Salzburg where she worked for an international boarding school. This is where she first met and fell in love with Pietro Borghesi, an event that would lead her to Pietro's Italy and their first restaurant together. It was a piadina shop in northern Italy where they served the traditional sandwich to appreciative locals.

The piadina style bread Sabrina learned to make more than 18 years ago in Italy can be enjoyed today at La Spiga. Each morning, the team begins the piadina, a unique grilled flatbread dough, and instantly, memories of Sabrina and Pietro's first restaurant float through on waves of aroma.

"I am a staunch traditionalist, even more so than my husband who is the only Italian in the family," laughed Sabrina. "Although I do believe that it's important to give the traditional foods a small twist to take it to the next level for the American public."

And that is what is so very special about La Spiga. Scarola Tiepida, fresh escarole salad, orange segments,

Photos Bob Peterson

Pass It On

"Pass cooking on to your child. You'll both be happier, healthier and enjoy life in a much different way."

—Sabrina Tinsley, chef-owner

toasted pistachios, golden raisins, taggiasca olives, and a warm "volpaia" red wine vinaigrette. Tagliatelle al Ragu with traditional Bolognese sauce. Salsiccia con l'Uva e Polenta, pork sausage braised with grapes, grilled polenta, montasio cheese and braised escarole. Petto d'Anatra Farcita, oven-roasted duck breast stuffed with prosciutto, sage, juniper, orange and roasted butternut squash. Lasagne di Melanzane, thinly sliced eggplant layered with house tomato sauce, béchamel, Parmigiano Reggiano.

And perhaps most notably famous, the Gnocchi al Pomodoro, Sabrina's potato gnocchi that's often referred to as "gossamer-light," is tossed in the signature La Spiga sauce and Parmigiano Reggiano—a favorite dish on Capital Hill, or anywhere.

When you're in the mood for homemade pasta that shines with the authentic spirit of Romagna, pay a visit to Osteria La Spiga. One day soon you might hear about their young new pastry chef.

PAPPARDELLE AL CONIGLIO
(Pappardelle Noodles with Braised Rabbit Sauce)

(Serves 6)

Pasta dough made with 6 eggs and 6 cups of unbleached all-purpose flour

- 1 onion, minced
- 1 carrot, minced
- 1 celery stalk, minced
- ¼ cup sage and rosemary, minced
- 4 slices prosciutto (or pancetta), julienned
- 2 Tbs olive oil
- 2 Tbs butter
- 1 cup white wine
- 2 cups rabbit or chicken stock
- 1 whole rabbit
  Flour for dusting
- ¼ cup Parmigiano Reggiano, grated

SAUCE

• Remove innards from the rabbit, conserve. • Quarter the rabbit, rinse it, and pat dry, salt and dust with flour.

• Make a quick stock with all innards except livers, using garlic, onion, celery, carrot.

• In a large pot, brown rabbit in oil and butter mixture then remove from pan.
• Add "soffritto" of onion, carrot and celery along with minced herbs to the pot, sauté until tender. • Add prosciutto or pancetta to the pot along with the minced livers and sauté to cook through. • Add rabbit back to pot, coat with the soffritto. • Add wine and allow to reduce, turning the rabbit once. • Add stock (rabbit, chicken or a combination of the two), bring to a boil, cover and reduce to a simmer.

• Allow to simmer until the meat is tender and pulls away from the bone (about 1 hour). • Cool slightly then remove the meat from the bones and

chop or shred to desired texture (save bones for stock if desired).

PASTA

• While the sauce is cooking, roll out your dough to desired thickness, allow to dry slightly, then cut into 1" wide pappardelle using a ravioli cutter.

• Cook the pasta in salted water. • Toss with the shredded rabbit meat and sauce and finish with Parmigiano.

SEATTLE · CAPITOL HILL

THE WHERE TO EAT GUIDE

BEND

As far as mountain towns go, Bend has it all. In the winter, a killer mountain that draws in skiers and snowboarders from all over the west. In the summer, a diverse river that fills with kayakers, paddle-boarders and whitewater enthusiasts. Amidst the outdoor adventure that captivates tourists and locals, there is a culinary scene that mirrors the fresh, organic, and full-of-heart spirit that fills this town.

You see, people who spend time in Bend quite simply love their life. The weather (300 days of sunshine a year), the Ponderosa pine-dusted air, the stunning Cascade Mountain peaks, the clear creeks that fall from waterfall to waterfall, the community of neighbors and business owners that support each other, the nightlife, the restaurants—Bend, the place, gives life to Bend, the people. They are a healthy brood; living life to the fullest and creatively making it work in what is, for them, the ideal locale.

Nowhere in Bend are people making it work quite as much as in the restaurant industry, where struggle and passion and hard work give birth to success. Bend is well-known nationwide for its micro-brew culture (and deservedly so), yet there is so much more than good beer and beer grub. Chefs, restaurateurs, wine experts, bartenders and servers are defining a style that is upscale and modern with just the right dose of mountain town gruff.

Bend restaurants are serving up dishes that reflect the healthy and elevated spirit of its people. Increasingly, they are sourcing ingredients from the wide-open lands and ranches east and north of town, giving new life to agricultural entrepreneurs and food artisans.

From its oldest restaurant resident, the Pine Tavern, to one of its newest, Spork, there is drive, camaraderie and creativity here. Sparked by the realities of tougher economic times, chefs and owners are dedicated to helping the local economy and each other. Bend knows what it's like to weather difficult times. As the economy begins to grow again, there is a feeling of "we're in this together" and a mentality that everyone deserves to succeed. Diners are loyal to the local model because they know they are supporting a friend or a neighbor or, at the very least, someone who knows and loves this town just as much as they do.

Add in the state-of-the-art culinary program at Central Oregon Community College's Cascade Culinary Institute and you have a recipe for a scene that is coming into its own and expanding to fill the type of heart that can only live in Bend--where a restaurant is not a commodity, but rather a sweet discovery of local spirit.

ARIANA RESTAURANT

W IT'S A TYPICAL TUESDAY MORNING
in mid-July on Bend's Westside. Galveston Avenue is just waking up to the sounds of delivery trucks and office commuters. A produce stand is setting out heirloom tomatoes, Rainier cherries and giant ruby peaches. The neighborhood brewpub looks quiet and tired from a night of servicing bronzed paddle boarders. There is a lazy hazy feel about this street on a summer morning – the kind of feeling you have as a kid on vacation. Nowhere to be. Not a care in the world.

Inside 1304 NW Galveston, however, a small family of passionate restaurateurs has already baked bread, finished sweet corn cookies for a cheesecake crust, received a fresh, wild Oregon Salmon directly from the fishermen who caught it, and lovingly put a pot of pork shanks in the oven to braise the day away with red wine.

There is a husband and wife meeting at the bar with notes and a reservation book. They live upstairs. There is a three year-old girl named Isabel sitting in a tall stool right next to her Papa.

This intimate 40-seat craftsmen bungalow, Ariana Restaurant, is much more than a successful restaurant that is a favorite for locals and tourists and booked most nights of the week. It is a family, quite literally, owned and managed by husband and wife Chefs Andres and Ariana Fernandez and Ariana's parents, Glenn and Susan Asti.

Andres and Ariana both grew up in households where the kitchen was an integral part of life and love. Andres was surrounded by the flavors of his mother and grandmother in Bogotá, Colombia where the food is colorful, fresh, handmade and ingrained in daily life. Ariana has early memories of her Italian father's now famous marinara sauce, and her grandparents' restaurant in Pittsburgh. "My mother, she always let me experiment in the kitchen as a child. She never cared if I made a mess," she said.

So, after attending culinary school, meeting, and marrying, Andres and Ariana decided to jump in and purchase a restaurant. They found the quaint bungalow on Galveston, then home to a popular coffee house, in 2004. Ten days after receiving the keys, Ariana Restaurant opened for business.

"It was strange that first night. We were surprised, and a little scared, to see people actually walk through the door," said Ariana.

Nine years later, after living through the economic bust that hit Bend so hard, at a time when it seemed like a restaurant was closing every day, Ariana is still putting out signature dishes. There is the Sicilian Style Calamari, a favorite of Chef Andres because it is never fried, made instead with tender rings and tentacles simmered in a slightly spicy tomato sauce with capers, currants, and toasted fregula. There is the Wild Oregon Line Caught Salmon, roasted, with baby shiitake mushrooms, creamed corn, fingerlings, and tamari. There is the Bone Marrow, roasted and served with rich beef reduction, parsley-spring onion salad and grilled bread, a dish that Bend diners might not readily order were it not for the loyal trust Ariana's followers put in the kitchen.

And that is perhaps the most alluring piece of Ariana's story, the loyal customers that come back time and time again – because they love the European bistro atmosphere, because they look forward to catching up with Susan at the door, because they'll see little Isabel grow and change with the seasons, because they admire Glenn's knowledge about Northwest wines, because they might run into Andres and Ariana at Paradise Produce picking the day's fruit and vegetables just a block from the restaurant, because they can request a server by name and know they'll suggest the very best – with the same passion and expertise as each time before.

"We never give up. We love food. We love our family. It's hard work, but it's a lot of fun, too," said Ariana.

As I popped into the warm and welcoming kitchen with Chef Ariana and tasted one of the sweet corn cookies she had baked before my arrival, her smile, the aroma of the braising pork shanks, and the perfectly soft and just slightly crisp cookie that burst with the flavor of a summer day told me exactly that.

CARAMELIZED JUMBO SEA SCALLOPS
with Dungeness Crab and Wild Shrimp Risotto

(Serves 4)

12	jumbo diver sea scallops
12	oz fresh lump Dungeness crab meat(cooked)
12	oz peeled and deveined shrimp, chopped (raw)
2	cups carnaroli risotto rice
½	cup dry white wine
2	large shallots, minced
4-5	cups shellfish stock or chicken stock
4	Tbs unsalted butter
½-1	cup Parmesan cheese, grated
2	Tbs Italian parsley, finely chopped
2	Tbs tarragon, finely chopped
1-3	tsp freshly squeezed lemon juice
3	Tbs canola or grapeseed oil
½	cup microgreens or picked herb leaves
	Kosher salt and freshly ground black pepper to taste

FOR RISOTTO

• In a large saucepan heat chicken or shellfish stock. • In another saucepan melt butter and sweat shallots over medium heat until soft and translucent. • Add carnaroli rice and stir to coat with butter, cook for about 3 minutes, stirring to prevent browning.

• Add wine to rice and cook until all liquid is absorbed. • Slowly ladle ½ cup stock into rice and stir frequently, as liquid is absorbed add another ½ cup. Keep stirring and adding stock until rice is fully cooked and has a creamy consistency. • Add chopped raw shrimp and cook 1 minute. • To finish add butter, cheese, crab, lemon juice, and chopped herbs. • Season with salt and pepper. Do not let risotto get too thick, keep it loose with more stock as it tends to tighten as it sits.

FOR SCALLOPS

• Heat a cast iron skillet until smoking. • Dry scallops on a paper towel, add canola oil to pan and carefully place scallops in hot oil. Do not move scallops for 2-3 minutes to ensure even caramelization. • Carefully scrape up scallops as they might stick and flip to cook the other side only briefly, about 30 seconds.

TO PLATE

• Spoon risotto into warmed bowls and top with seared scallops. • Garnish with microgreens or picked herbs.

JACKSON'S CORNER

AT JACKSON'S CORNER, IT'S PRETTY simple: Surround yourself with good food and community. Repeat as often as possible.

Whether you're a visitor walking in for the first time or a regular who lives on the next block, the moment you walk into the corner building at 845 NW Delaware Avenue, you are immediately at home.

Perhaps it's because of the history. Since its beginnings as a small grocer in the 1920s, this address has brought the neighborhood together around food. It's the kind of history you can feel.

Perhaps it's because of the house-made pasta made fresh every day with local, organic eggs. Maybe it's the pizza, baked in a brick oven in the middle of their open kitchen and topped with local greens and meats. It could be the short, European-style wine glasses that invite comfort and casual merry-making. Perhaps it's because of the staff who is always happy, always knowledgeable, and really in love with

the work they do.

Or maybe it's a combination of all of these fantastic factors that come together to create something intrinsically beautiful inside what locals often refer to lovingly as "Jackson's" or "The Corner."

"We have a passion for eating good food and doing something positive for the community," said Aaron Christenson, co-owner and general manager.

And that is exactly what Jackson's Corner has been doing since its opening in 2008. When Jay Junkin, co-owner, decided to revive the iconic corner he asked himself, "What can we bring to the neighborhood?" Jay was already running a successful taco and burrito shack called Parrilla Grill in another section of Bend's Westside. He was in a pretty comfortable position and didn't need to focus on making this second endeavor thrive. Instead, he was able to focus on the neighborhood and bringing people together. He wanted it to grow organically from the needs of the neighborhood and meet a demand that only a local market café could meet.

You might say that's where the magic lives.

Jay brought in large wooden tables with benches and chairs you'd find in your grandmother's kitchen. He kept the market theme by including a wall of coolers stocked with beer, wine and other tasty beverages. He used chalkboards to announce the specials of the day. He didn't hire wait staff; instead he brought customers to the front counter where they could see the kitchen. He sent his chef to the Downtown Bend Farmers Market with a shopping cart to pick the best of the day's harvest—an idea that led to the creation of their Market Salad.

With the help of Aaron Christensen, co-owner and general manager, Jackson's Corner continues to focus on sourcing local products whenever possible. While the chef no longer shops at the Bend Farmers Market every week, Jackson's Corner instead sources from local community supported agriculture (CSA) to fill the needs of their

high volume breakfast, lunch and dinner crowds. This is an important piece of the sustainable, neighborhood-focused puzzle that connects the restaurant directly to the predominantly local, organic farmers and ranchers that fill the menu.

This community-filled space is a clear favorite in town, and what adds to the warm feelings and charming atmosphere is that you could, if you wanted to, stay here all day. Start the day with the Corner Cristo. The French toast will remind you of your mother's only better because of local bacon, an organic egg and gruyere cheese. Enjoy a Jackson's Bleu salad for lunch, packed with organic greens, organic apples, candied walnuts and bleu cheese vinaigrette. Finish the day sharing a bottle of red or Earl Grey Sodas made with tea, muddled spearmint, soda and gin, and a brick oven pizza topped with marinara, sopressetta sausage, mozzarella and provolone cheeses, and local organic arugula.

Sounds good, you say? We'll see you at the Corner.

MUSHROOM PANCETTA PASTA

(Serves 4)

- ¼ cup oil
- 4 cups mushrooms (crimini, oyster, chanterelle, or a mix!)
- 1 cup diced pancetta
- ¼ cup chopped garlic
- ¼ cup chopped shallot
- ½ cup Marsala
- 2-3 cups of heavy cream (just enough to almost cover the mushrooms in pan)
- 6-8 cups cooked pasta

• Heat a large sauté pan over medium-high heat, add oil. • When oil is hot, add mushrooms and cook until golden brown. • Add pancetta and cook until brown. • Add garlic and shallot, tossing often until golden. • Deglaze with Marsala and reduce by half.

• Add cream to barely cover mushrooms (add more or less depending on how saucy you like it!) • Reduce cream until a caramel color appears around the edges. • Add your favorite cooked pasta, toss with the sauce and serve!

Photos Ariel Dawn Photography

BRICKHOUSE

JUST PAST THE MAÎTRE D' STAND, there is a quiet dedication on a lone brick wall:

> *his laugh rings out —*
> *no need for the fisherman*
> *to exaggerate.*
>   -haiku by Francine Porad

Alongside the poem, there is a photo of a man on a dock holding a 70.5-pound King Salmon. He is laughing out loud as only a prize-winning fisherman would do. The photo is so palpable you can almost hear his laughter ring across the other brick walls that circumvent this popular downtown Bend eatery.

The picture, of Brickhouse owners Jeff and Bruce Porad's father, is more than a dedication to a father and fisherman that passed away several years ago; it is indicative of everything that Jeff and his wife Jodi aim to do with this restaurant. Fresh food. Family. Laughter.

When Jeff was a young boy growing up in the Puget Sound area of Seattle, his father Bernie would wake him up at 2 or 3 o'clock in the morning to fish. Jeff was forced off with a crab pot in one hand and a clam-digging shovel in the other. Steelhead, salmon, clams, oysters, Dungeness crab—these were the flavors, and work requirements, of Jeff's childhood. While he was reticent to give up sleep and venture out into the early-morning hours, the experience made an impact that can be seen in his restaurant today.

"I earned a passion for fresh seafood. One day out of the water, and it was on our plates, most times even sooner. Not farm-raised, never frozen," said Jeff.

After spending time working at restaurants throughout the Northwest, Jeff and Jodi settled in Redmond, Oregon where they opened the steak and seafood house that now boasts a second location in Bend. The Bend restaurant made a highly anticipated move in the spring of 2013 to downtown's iconic red brick fire hall on the corner of Lava and Minnesota. The 120-seat Bend restaurant is spacious, warm and inviting. In the summer it opens up to an additional 40 seats out on Minnesota Avenue by way of full-length French doors and leather seating out on the sidewalk. In the winter, a back room sits warm and ablaze with a fireplace that Jodi envisions as the perfect après ski destination for discerning steak lovers.

Ah, yes, the steaks. The steaks at Brickhouse are something spectacular in Central Oregon, sourced from natural Northwest farms. All are center-cut, custom-aged and hormone-free. Brickhouse serves only the highest choice beef and will gladly cut a larger size to order. Perhaps the most-favored preparation is the Filet Oscar, a beef tenderloin dressed with Dungeness crab, asparagus and béarnaise. The Blackened Rib Eye, cut to 12 oz or 16 oz (or larger should you desire) is another favorite. If you're looking for something a little more luxurious, there is always the American Kobe Beef (Wagyu) from Snake River Farms, cut as a filet mignon or New York strip—a fantastic treat.

And Bernie, Jeff's father, would be pleased to know that the seafood is as fresh as Jeff was used to as a boy. "In the water one day, on our plates the next," still rings true. Jeff has relationships with a bevvy of local Northwest fisherman in the summer and in the winter focuses on warm water exotic fish that can be shipped overnight.

The cocktails are as crisp and classic as the food. A Manhattan made with high-end vermouth is of course popular, as is the Cucumber Martini that sings with freshly squeezed juices and muddled basil. The wine program is accessible, approachable and regional on one end, and trophy on the other. "We like to support our neighbors first," said Jeff, which means Brickhouse has a fair selection of Northwest wines. They also boast a room that includes first-growth Bordeaux and a collection of impressive vintages.

Outside of the high-quality ingredients and expert preparations, it is Jodi's hospitality that sets Brickhouse apart. "We try to be family to everyone that walks in the door," she said.

The next time you visit Brickhouse for dinner, be sure to find Bernie's plaques on the wall. They tell you everything you need to know about this restaurant, this family. And then proceed to have one of the very best steaks in Central Oregon.

FILET OSCAR

(Serves 6)

6	6-8 oz tenderloin filets
24	spears of asparagus – steamed
16	oz fresh Dungeness crab meat
12	oz Bearnaise Sauce
	Extra virgin olive oil
	Salt and pepper

• Brush tenderloins with olive oil.

• Season well with salt and pepper.
• Grill or sear filets to desired temperature. • Allow filets to rest a minute before adding the Oscar. • When filet is done resting, top with 4 spears of asparagus, 2 oz of Bearnaise sauce and 2-3 oz Dungeness crab meat.

BEARNAISE SAUCE

1	lemon, juiced
4	egg yolks
2	dashes Tabasco sauce
	Salt and pepper to taste
¼	cup water
½	cup clarified butter
1	Tbs Tarragon Reduction **

• In a double boiler on medium heat whisk together lemon juice, egg yolks, Tabasco, salt and pepper and water until slightly thick and opaque. • Remove from heat and emulsify with clarified butter.

• Stir in Tarragon Reduction. • Adjust seasoning to taste.

**TARRAGON REDUCTION

1	Tbs dry tarragon
1	tsp shallots
1	oz red wine
2	oz red wine vinegar

• In a small sauce pan bring all ingredients to a slow boil. • Reduce heat and allow to simmer until excess liquid is gone. • Cool to room temperature before adding to sauce.

900 WALL

The menu rotates with seasonally appropriate dishes that reflect a strong Italian influence and a focus on locally sourced products. House-made charcuterie. Local grass fed beef, lamb and local cheeses. A shifting vegetable section that highlights 900 Wall's commitment to cooking in regard to the season. An abundance of gluten-free and vegetarian dishes that don't make dietary restrictions feel like an afterthought, but rather a genuine attention to guests' needs and enjoyment.

And the wine – oh the wine. More than 50 by the glass, many from the Northwest region, plus six sparkling selections by the glass. An interesting and robust bottle menu consisting of more than 200 cellar offerings, winning 900 Wall the *Wine Spectator* Award of Excellence 2 years running.

Perhaps one of the more alluring things about the 900 Wall design has to do with the way Eslinger quietly cares for his staff, his guests and his community.

ASK ANY BEND LOCAL ABOUT THE

beautiful, awning-laden brick building on the corner of Wall Street and Minnesota Avenue, and they will invariably tell you a story of food and friendship.

You'll hear about the wine program, the happy hour, the local ingredients and produce-driven philosophy that has made 900 Wall one of the most well-known and loved restaurants in Bend since its opening in 2009.

You'll also likely hear that 900 Wall is, by far, the best place in town to meet a friend for a glass of wine.

And if the story really gets to the heart of the matter, you'll hear about the chef who helped build this restaurant from the ground up.

"A restaurant is not easy to run, and even harder to open," said 900 Wall Executive Chef Cliff Eslinger.

That's something Eslinger, the quietly astute chef that is behind the success story at 900 Wall, knows quite a bit about. He has seen restaurants come and go throughout his time on the restaurant scene in Bend, and has been an integral part of some of the most favored since moving to Bend in 2001.

But it is his menu design at 900 Wall that has put a permanently stellar mark on the career of this Culinary Institute of America trained chef – a design that focuses on locally driven, sustainable, high-quality ingredients and dishes that change with the seasons; a design that has earned him distinction as one of the 10 regional chefs highlighted in the *Best Chefs America Book*.

Relationships with your farmer, butcher, cheese monger and produce stocker are invaluable. Their knowledge is endless and can make a huge difference in what you cook because they want to sell you the ripest or most seasonally appropriate item. They may also take the time to turn you on to a product that they're fired up on that you would have never discovered if they didn't value your relationship. You just need to foster those relationships.

—Executive Chef Cliff Eslinger

"We're a small town. We've been through rough times. We have to take care of the people who take care of us," he said.

He extends this idea to the servers, bartenders and kitchen crews who found themselves out of work during the toughest of economic times in Bend; to the local artisans, purveyors and farmers that are now seeing success in and around the high desert of Central Oregon; to restaurant owners and chefs that have come and gone.

900 Wall has helped put Bend on the map in terms of sustainable, approachable cuisine. And clearly, Chef Eslinger, who grew up amongst the farms and artisans of Upstate New York, has a lot to do with continuing the trend in the region.

WARM KALE SALAD

1   loaf of crusty sourdough
2   bunches Lacinato kale, also known as Tuscan kale
3   cups cherry tomatoes
2   medium sized eggplant
½   cup coarsely grated Pecorino Romano
1   cup vegetable stock
¾   cup Calabrian Chile Vinaigrette

Photos Red Owl Photography

• Make the Calabrian Chile Vinaigrette recipe below first. • Once the vinaigrette is complete, set the oven to broil.

• Cut 3 cups of 1" croutons from the loaf of bread and toss with salt, pepper and a generous amount of extra virgin olive oil. • Cut the eggplant into 1" pieces with the skin left on and toss with salt, pepper and a generous amount of extra virgin olive oil. • Toss the tomatoes with extra virgin olive oil and place under the broiler until they split and are lightly charred, then set aside somewhere warm.

• Set the oven to 425°

• Roast the eggplant at 425° until starting to caramelize around the edges. • Remove from the oven and set somewhere warm. • While the eggplant is roasting put the croutons in the oven and cook until they are browned but still chewy in the center. • While the croutons and eggplant are in the oven put 2 large saute pans over medium high heat on the stove. • Once the pans are hot, add half of the vinaigrette and half of the vegetable stock to each pan and bring to a simmer.

• Once the liquid begins to simmer add half the kale and half the eggplant to each pan and stir while cooking to wilt the kale by half its original volume.

• Divide the croutons, pecorino and tomatoes between each pan and toss.

CALABRIAN CHILE VINAIGRETTE

1½   cup extra virgin olive oil
¼   cup Calabrian chiles, seeded and sliced thin

1   Tbs oil packed anchovy filets chopped very fine
¼   cup garlic sliced thin
1   cup yellow onion julienne
1   cup red wine vinegar
2   tsp black pepper finely ground

• Cook the chiles and anchovies in the oil over medium heat. • Once the chiles turn brick red in color, add the garlic and onion and cook until tender.

• Add vinegar, black pepper and salt.

• Cool.

CHOW

CHOW. SOMETIMES A NAME SAYS it all. Good, simple food that supports the local economy. This has been chef-owner David Touvell's goal since Chow's opening day.

And if you live in Bend, chances are, the charming bungalow on the corner of Newport Avenue and NW 11th Street is one of your very favorite places to eat.

Open for breakfast and lunch, Chow offers the best of locally sourced ingredients, many of which come from their own backyard. Nine raised beds and an additional 400 square-feet of space complete the Chow kitchen garden and make it easy to see why Chow is able to do local and sustainable really well.

The next time you're at Chow during the growing season, take a peek at their gardens. Packed with leafy greens like spinach and kale, as well as squashes, tomatoes, radishes, and a bounty of herbs, the garden supplies the Chow kitchen with hyper-local resources throughout the summer and early fall. Chow also partners with local schools to educate students about gardening and the economic benefits to the local community.

Because of his work at Chow, David is known as one of the pioneers of the local food movement in Bend, and with good reason. In addition to his on-site garden, Chow partners with more than twenty local purveyors for everything from meats and cheeses to tea. Cada Dia Cheese, Juniper Grove Cheese, DD Ranch, Bendistillery, Townshend's Tea, Metolius Tea & Apothecary, as well as a selection of Bend's finest beers -- these connections help build beautiful plates, many of which are vegetarian and vegan-friendly.

On the other side of the bungalow, you'll find a delightful patio space that seats happy diners in fair weather. On the weekends, live music is always on deck, which when passersby notice from Newport Avenue, makes Chow look like the best party in town.

But the real magic happens in the kitchen where

Photos Red Owl Photography

French discipline is understated, creativity is fresh, and local products are given the best attention. Chow co-owner Shawn Harvey recommends one of Bend's favorite poached egg presentations that come together here: The Blackstone, poached eggs, corn meal crusted tomatoes, spinach, bacon, Béarnaise sauce, and The Sampson, poached eggs, crab cakes, sauce Choron. The pancakes are homemade and hot off the griddle and offer diners choices of Pumpkin & Ginger, Toasted Oatmeal & Multigrain or Buttermilk. The House-made Buttermilk Biscuits smothered in 4 styles of gravy (country style, red

eye, veggie sausage, or chorizo) are another popular dish. An extensive "Alternative and Additions" menu makes dietary restrictions enjoyable: sautéed tofu or corn meal crusted tomatoes with sea salt can substitute meat on any dish, breakfast or lunch.

At lunch, the Crispy Crab Sandwich is a local favorite. House-made bread is layered with crispy crab, avocado, greens, farmer's bacon, and aioli—it's the most textural, flavorful sandwich you'll have.

For David, the idea of a sustainable, local restaurant really started when he was just nine years old. While 'working' at an organic bakery in Ventura, California, he learned the art of dough making and quickly figured out how to master it his own way. Those early bakery moments, filled with creativity, play and idealism, lead him on to a stellar chef career including Mobile 5-star restaurants and James Beard award-winning restaurants all along the west coast. But he kept coming back to the ideas he was taught as a young boy.

"Essentially, I found myself in Bend and I needed to decide if I was going to continue someone else's vision or go my own way. Clearly, I wanted to go my own way," laughed David. Bend is so happy that he did.

EGGS BLACKSTONE

(Serves 4)

The difference between Eggs Blackstone and the better-known Eggs Benedict is that the former calls for bacon instead of ham. A ripe, juicy tomato, maybe one of the heirloom varieties such as Brandywine or Marvel Stripe, makes this special brunch dish stellar, but any tomato variety may be used.

BÉARNAISE SAUCE

1 Tbs chopped fresh tarragon leaves
2 shallots, minced
¼ cup red wine vinegar
¼ cup red wine
3 egg yolks
⅛ cup white wine
8 oz butter, melted and clarified
¼ tsp salt
¼ tsp cayenne pepper
½ fresh lemon, squeezed

Make the shallot and tarragon reduction first. • In a small saucepan, combine the tarragon, chopped shallots, vinegar and wine over medium-high heat. • Bring to a simmer and cook until reduced by half. • Remove from heat and set aside to cool.

• Blend egg yolks and 1/8 cup white wine in a heat-safe bowl or top of a double boiler. • Continue to whisk together over a pan of simmering water until foaming and thick. • Add clarified butter while continuing to whisk until emulsified. • Season with salt, cayenne pepper, lemon juice and shallot reduction. • If the sauce seems too thick at this point, add a small amount of hot water. • Set aside in a warm spot to hold the sauce.

BUILDING THE BLACKSTONE

8 thick bacon slices, cut in half
1 tsp fresh lemon juice
8 eggs
8 heirloom or regular tomato slices
  Freshly ground black pepper, to taste
1 lb fresh spinach

• Preheat a broiler.

• Arrange the bacon slices in a single layer on a baking sheet and place in the broiler about 6 inches from the heat source. • Broil the slices until browned, about 3 minutes. • Turn the slices over and broil until browned on the other side, about 2 minutes more. • Transfer the bacon to paper towels to drain.

• Pour water to a depth of 2 inches into a large fry pan and add the lemon juice. • Set over medium heat and bring to a gentle simmer. • Break 1 egg into a small bowl or cup. • Hold the bowl so it is just touching the simmering water and slide the egg into the water. • Quickly repeat with the remaining eggs, one at a time, keeping them about 1 inch apart. • Adjust the heat to keep the water at a gentle simmer. • Cook until the whites are set and the yolks are glazed over but still soft, 4 to 5 minutes.

• About 1 minute before the eggs are done, sauté spinach in butter. • Top each tomato slice with equal parts spinach and two bacon slices per plate. • Using a slotted spoon, lift each egg from the simmering water, letting the excess water drain into the pan. • Trim any ragged edges of egg white with kitchen scissors. • Top each tomato half with 1 poached egg and sprinkle with black pepper. • Spoon 2 tablespoons of the Béarnaise sauce over each egg. • Serve immediately.

PINE TAVERN

🍴 WOMEN BUILT THE PINE TAVERN – two very enterprising women – in 1936.

At a time when the country was just beginning to pull itself out of the Great Depression and Bend was growing a community of timber industry workers and their families, it is somewhat remarkable to think of Maren Gribskov and Eleanor Bechen, two women who quickly became known as the best cooks and hosts in Central Oregon.

They were quite the savvy business owners as well, running the iconic restaurant for almost thirty years.

Now, almost seven decades later, and after switching hands only four times, the Pine Tavern is still operated by a pair of women, Justine Bender Bennett and her mother Christine Bender.

"The Pine Tavern is about prudence and knowing your history," said Justine. "It is about good American eats, home cooking and comfort in knowing that your favorite dish is going to be the same the next time you come back."

The Chicken Pot Pie with carrots, peas, onions, mushrooms, potatoes, garlic, shallots, and puff pastry stirs memories and comforts of home. The Pine Tavern Meatloaf with Oregon mushroom demi, mashed potatoes and seasonal vegetables is classic and full of warmth. The 12 oz Angus Rib eye from Northwest ranchers is "one of the very best steaks in Bend," said Justine.

But it is the Sourdough Scones with honey butter that earn more raves and flat-out obsessions than any other item on the menu. Justine's father, Bert Bender, adopted this traditional Basque recipe while at the legendary Warm Springs Ranch in Ketchum, Idaho. When he purchased the Pine Tavern in the early 1980s, he brought the popular scones with him, and folks all over the Northwest thank the skies up above that he did. They're that good, and they're just the same today as they were back then. Sinful, buttery, and—some say—better tasting than a donut.

Many say that you have not truly experienced Bend without enjoying a meal at the Pine Tavern. In the summer, the patio offers stunning views of the Deschutes River and Mirror Pond. In the winter, there is nothing more classically beautiful than the curtained shutters and warm glowing windows that beckon guests on Brooks Street.

A Tree Grows In It

The most talked-about features of the Pine Tavern are the two towering pine trees that grow right through the middle of the dining room. Up through the roof they go, into the brilliant Central Oregon sky. A fitting trademark in a restaurant and town whose roots are so firmly planted in the plight of the pine tree.

For Justine, the experience is much more personal. She fondly remembers days exploring the restaurant as a young child. Feeding the ducks with breadcrumbs leftover from lunch service, binging on sourdough scones to the point of illness, and the many wonderful employees who looked after her like their own.

"My dad created a family of loyal staff and happy customers, and we're continuing that tradition. We've been a part of this community for decades, and we hope to be a part of it for many more," said Justine.

Sourdough-scone-loving, prime-rib-adoring fans all over the Northwest and beyond surely hope the same.

DUNGENESS CRAB CAKE

Julie Halterman

¼ cup yellow onion, minced
¼ tsp minced fresh garlic
¼ cup minced celery
2 Tbs fine chopped parsley
1 oz Dijon mustard
½ oz Worcestershire sauce
3½ oz mayonnaise
1½ lbs Dungeness crab
3 whole eggs
½ sleeve Saltine crackers
¼ Tbs butter

• Peel and mince yellow onion, garlic and celery. • Remove leaves from parsley stems and chop fine.

• Combine the minced vegetables with the mayonnaise, Dijon mustard and Worchestershire sauce.

• Beat the eggs for 1 minute or until pale in color.

• Break up the crackers into small pieces (not dust) and add them to the egg mixture.

• Remove as much liquid as possible from the crab and fold into mixture.

• Place mixture into fridge before use.

• In a non-stick skillet over medium heat add ¼ Tbs of butter. • Place a 2 oz ball of the Dungeness crab cake mixture into the skillet. Once golden brown on one side flip over and press ball down to form cake. Once golden brown on both sides remove from skillet and let rest.

• On a serving plate, place ½ oz of the lemon pepper vinaigrette down,

position hot crab cake on vinaigrette and garnish with a salad of fresh arugula.

LEMON PEPPER VINAIGRETTE

2 oz fresh lemon juice
¼ oz Dijon mustard
Pinch kosher salt
Pinch ground black pepper
6 oz extra virgin olive oil
¼ tsp fresh thyme
¼ tsp shallot minced
¼ oz granulated sugar

• Remove leaves from thyme sprigs and chop fine.

• Place the thyme, Dijon mustard, lemon juice, minced shallots, salt and pepper into a blender and blend. • Slowly add extra virgin olive oil until well emulsified.

BEND • DOWNTOWN

TIM GARLING'S JACKALOPE GRILL

Ellotte (Ellie) Garling

DOWNTOWN • BEND

THERE ARE TWO THINGS YOU
need to know about Chef Tim Garling: One, he likes to become an expert at everything he does. Two, he tends to have a great deal of fun while earning that expertise.

"Everything I do, I try to become an expert, but occasionally I like to be tongue-in-cheek about it," laughs Tim.

This is evidenced by his demeanor with the guests of his downtown Bend restaurant, Jackalope Grill, by the way he laughs with his daughter Ellie, by the way he has a love of hosting dinner parties where sushi and champagne flow freely, and if you look very close at his menu, by the way he plays with words in entrees such as General Sam's Hoisin Glazed Game Hen Salad—a nod to his sous chef, Sam.

Tim's search for culinary expertise began many years ago while on a bike trip through the south of France. That initial trip, where he learned the smells and sounds of the French countryside, would bring him to culinary school at La Varenne in Paris for two years. He was lured back often, he figures 15-20 times, to Paris, the Loire Valley, the city of Bordeaux and he came to know these places well, and the influence on his cooking is apparent.

But what some might not know is that it was an 11-month trip from Luxembourg to Nepal that left an indelible mark on the way he thinks about food.

"My ex-wife and I quit our jobs and hitchhiked all the way from Luxembourg through the Middle East. We ate at bakeries in Afghanistan. I developed an affinity for the flavors and culture and I started to think about latitudes and how they share ingredients and influence. How flavors that you taste in the Southwestern United States are shared with profiles in certain parts of Asia," said Tim.

Now, he sees that influence he found long ago in one of his favorite dishes at Jackalope—his Columbia River King Salmon. Caught by dipnet fishermen of the Warm Springs tribe via an ancient fishing technique still in use today along the Upper Deschutes River north of Bend, the salmon is cured with brown sugar, alder-smoked, and then served hot on top of buckwheat Japanese Soba noodles in a soy-mushroom-sesame broth with fresh shiitake mushrooms. Its Asian influence is clear and somewhat surprising on a menu that is mostly French and classically influenced, but as you taste notes of kefir lime and lemongrass and sake, it makes sense within the context of Tim's style, persona and interpretations of latitudinal flavors.

Kathy Garling, Tim's wife and the better half of the restaurant, had a big hand in the creation of this salmon dish. She also plays a big role in most facets of the front of the house as host—keeping guests welcomed and happy and pleasantly entertained, assuring that the servers and bartenders are knowledgeable and attentive, and designing a space, both inside and out, that is sophisticated and classy without feeling pretentious.

As you wander through the 65-seat dining room during

Cooking should give you pleasure. You should enjoy cooking with family and friends, sharing the experience and perhaps a bottle of wine or a craft beer. Relax, enjoy and have fun with this. Good home cooking is the enemy of junk food and processed food. Make the world better one dish at a time.

—Tim Garling, owner and executive chef

---

the summer months, you'll find a magical oasis towards the back, a gorgeous courtyard where herb boxes overflow with tarragon and basil and rosemary and nasturtium, where globe lights twinkle in the sky as dusk falls, and where live music gently radiates on certain summer nights.

On Tim's constantly changing menu you'll find several of his classic and most-favored dishes—the Escargot à la Bourguignonne that garnered a cult following quite quickly, the Grilled Prawns & Chickpea Panisse that surprise with Tim's chickpea fries, the Steamed Totten Inlet Mussels Marinières that lures you in with perfectly opened mussels and a broth that is best savored with the table's Sparrow Baker bread, the Jaeger Schnitzel that is, well, just perfect, and the Cascade Farms All Natural Pork Osso Bucco that recalls seasons and Europe and love all in one decadent dish.

When asked why he ventured into cooking in the first place, Tim laughs again as he explains, "At the beginning, it was more or less to enable me to entertain friends. Now the food is all about self-expression. When you hit that resonance, that's what I'm looking for."

MEDALLIONS OF PORK TENDERLOIN
Braised with Sun-Dried Cherries, Jalapeño Chiles, Balsamic Vinegar and Apple Cider

(Serves 4)

2   Tbs olive oil
2   lb pork tenderloin denuded and cut into 12, 2 ounce medallions (see chef's notes)
1   cup concentrated apple cider (see chef's notes)
1   cup balsamic vinegar (see chef's notes)
32 sundried Montmorency cherries
2   medium jalapeños, deseeded and cut into a julienne
    Flour for dredging
    Parsley, chives and/or scallions finely minced for garnishing

• Preheat oven to 300°

• Sprinkle the medallions with salt and pepper. Dredge one side of the medallion with flour. (Shake off the excess flour.) • Heat the olive oil in heavy sauté pan over medium-high heat.

• Place the floured side of the medallion into the hot oil and cook the medallions until brown on both sides. Remove to a warm serving platter. Keep the platter and medallions warm in a low oven.

• Pour out excess oil and then put the vinegar, cider, cherries and jalapeño julienne into the hot pan. Reduce by half.

• Add the warm medallions back to the sauté pan along with any accumulated juices. Cook, turning several times until they are done to your satisfaction.

• Remove the medallions to a warm platter; reduce the sauce to a syrup.

• Pour the sauce over the medallions evenly distributing the jalapeño and the cherries. • Garnish with chopped parsley or scallions and serve immediately.

Chef's Notes:

⑃ I usually figure about 6 oz of pork per person (3 ea 2 oz medallions). A large tenderloin will generally yield about two servings (3 medallions per person).

⑃ Despite the liberal use of jalapeño you will find only a modest amount of spicy heat from them. Of course, this is only true if the seeds are removed and the chile is well cleaned. If you'd like the dish more spicy, leave some of the seeds in.

⑃ Try to find a not too sweet fresh cider. Apples grown in a cooler environment work best. But, to use fresh cider, you must boil it down to the original volume (and strain it) before proceeding with the recipe.

⑃ Don't use your best 20-year-old balsamic vinegar for this! (A few drops of that 20+ year old over the finished dish would be nice, however!) Just use the regular (Aceto Balsamico di Modena) and not an expensive grade.

Jackalope Grill

SPORK

IF YOU TAKE A CLOSE look at the front counter of Spork's new 50-seat space on Newport Avenue, you'll see clever nods to a time gone by.

Sheets of rounded, knotted steel lay the foundation to the counter and remind loyal fans of "the Airstream," Spork's wildly popular mobile food cart that fed Bend for four years before going brick and mortar in June 2013.

Spork started as a globally inspired green-conscious, veggie-friendly mobile streetfood kitchen. Bendites lined up for pork carnitas, grilled corn, and a spicy fried chicken that made grown men cry. They won "Best Of" awards from local media every single year. Their bright green logo and playful name translated to rocking flavors, creative people and uniquely good times.

Clearly, co-owners Jeff Hunt and Erica Reilly had a good thing going, but there was an inherent limitation in running a mobile kitchen. Then a space on the westside called their name. They answered.

Inspired by global kitchens in Portland, such as Pok Pok and Bollywood Theater (see page 34), Jeff and Erica worked with local designers, woodworkers and architects to create a space that is full of energy and positive vibes. The moment you walk in the space, you feel as if you've traveled to a far-off land, a land where bamboo mixes with stainless steel, where colors pop and inspire, where music rolls around and thumps in your heart, where flavors present themselves with a unique beauty and character that is all Spork.

The food is, of course, a big part of the story. Jeff, with roots at Marz Bistro and the much-adored The Grove, is still turning out the signature dishes that garnered a loyal street following, fusing flavors from across Latin America, Asia and beyond, covered and remixed in delightful ways.

Favorites, like the Spicy Fried Chicken, a rice flour battered boneless fried chicken served with spicy sweet sambal chile sauce, green onion, toasted sesame and jasmine rice, are just as tasty as they've always been. You'll also find Lomo Saltado, a Hoisin Pork Belly Sando, Yellow Curry Catfish, and some of the best tacos in Bend.

Spork's craft cocktails will also take you on a journey of the senses. Erica, aka "the Cocktail Maven," has put together a cocktail menu inspired by a classic cocktail revival of sorts. The Singapore Sling, the recipe that Erica says "really blew my skirt up" combines gin with fresh lime, Benedictine (a French herbal liquor), Cherry Heering and soda. Erica's cocktails are unlike anything you'll find in Bend. Fresh, flavorful, and complimenting the spirit, they are drinks to savor and you are encouraged to pay attention to every sip.

Within the new brick and mortar design, food and cocktails, you'll still find that friendly and positive spirit that makes Spork, Spork—which really, at its heart, couldn't take itself too seriously.

Citrus Power

Use more citrus! By adding a bit of citrus to a dish or a drink, you balance out the flavors in a beautiful way.

—Erica Reilly, co-owner

LOMO SALTADO

(Serves 4)

This is a popular Peruvian dish that shows a Chinese influence, combining steak and potatoes with rice and soy and stir-fry cooking.

- 1 lb beef tenderloin
- 1 lb red potato
- 4 eggs (optional)
- Crème fraîche (optional)
- 1 large red bell pepper
- 1 large red onion
- 2 cups steamed jasmine rice
- Salt and pepper to taste
- Olive oil

• Place the potatoes in a small sauce pan with cold water and salt and simmer until easily pierced with a knife but not too soft. You want them to be firm.

• While the potatoes cook drizzle the tenderloin and tomatoes with a small amount of olive oil, season with salt and pepper, and fire up a grill. We like a charcoal grill with mesquite hardwood charcoal but any will do.

• Grill the tomatoes until lightly charred. Set aside for the tomato purée. • Grill the tenderloin until very rare and let rest.

GINGER SOY

- 8 oz soy sauce
- 4 oz mirin
- 3 oz brown sugar
- 1 oz minced garlic
- 1 oz minced ginger
- 1 oz sliced green onion

• Make the ginger soy by combining the soy sauce, mirin, ginger, garlic, and green onion in a small sauce pan on low heat and whisk until the sugar is dissolved.

TOMATO PURÉE

- 1 lb vine ripened tomato

- ¼ cup extra virgin olive oil
- ½ oz minced garlic
- 1 oz minced shallot
- 1 Tbs kosher salt
- 1 tsp toasted and ground black pepper

• Make the tomato purée. • In a blender, food processer, or hand blender combine the charred tomatoes, the olive oil, garlic, shallot, salt, and pepper and purée until smooth.

• Thinly slice the tenderloin against the grain. • Cut the potatoes in half lengthwise and then slice into ¼" thick pieces. • Julienne the bell pepper and red onion.

• Cook the eggs. We like ours sunny side up.

• While cooking the eggs heat some olive oil in a 12" wok or large sauté pan. • Once the oil is very hot fry the potatoes until golden brown and deliciously crispy. • Add the onions and peppers to the pan. Keep everything moving in the wok and cook until soft and starting to brown. • Add the sliced tenderloin to the wok and continue to cook on high heat for another minute. • Add the tomato purée and cook until it starts to caramelize, about a minute. • Add the ginger soy. • Reduce the sauce. It should be fairly wet but not overly saucy.

GARNISH

Sliced radish
Thinly sliced green onion
Lime wedges

• Serve with the steamed jasmine rice, top with fried eggs, and a little crème fraîche. • Garnish with a lime wedge, some sliced green onion, and some sliced radish. Enjoy!

Photos Amy Castano

THE VICTORIAN CAFÉ

There's also the Man-Mosa, a super-sized version of their mimosa, made with private label Victorian Café Champagne and served in a pint glass with fresh orange juice.

Today, The Vic serves more than 75,000 people each year in a space that sits just 40 guests.

They feast on the food as much as the experience, which makes John very, very happy.

"That's what separates a good restaurant from a great restaurant. Turning the meal into an experience," said John.

At The Vic, the meal is important, along with the gourmet cocktails, fun-loving staff and charming dark-wood dining room and outdoor patio. For the last four years, Chef Josh Podwils has been making flavorful benedicts that appeal to every taste. The combinations include the Classic with Canadian bacon; the California with sliced hormone-free turkey, bacon, fresh spinach and avocado; the Bristol Bay with fresh seafood cakes; the Texas Hold'em with spicy BBQ pulled pork, sautéed onions and green chiles; the Caribbean with Cuban seasoned ham, mango, black beans and fresh cilantro; and the Roasted Veggie with squash, zucchini, mushrooms, onions and roasted tomatoes. All are served with homemade, grilled English muffins, hollandaise and two farm-fresh poached eggs.

Photos Douglas Miller

There are also omelets, pancakes, and a gourmet French toast that gets coated in Graham cracker crust, and then egg grilled and topped with homemade sauce, fresh fruit and whipping crème.

And that's just breakfast! The Vic is also open for lunch, and while the breakfast menu remains during the lunch

THERE IS A MOMENT OF THANKS

that comes when drinking a Bloody Mary in front of the fire pit at The Victorian Café.

That first sip, surrounded by friends and neighbors, warmth and brunch aromas, on a lazy weekend morning—you take that first sip and can't help but think, "Thank you universe. Life is so incredibly good right now."

Next time you're thanking the universe for that exceptional moment, we recommend that you also thank John Nolan, owner of The Victorian Café.

After all, it was John who reclaimed not only the spirit and potential of what locals now call The Vic, but also the outstanding bar program that makes "the breakfast worth waiting for" all the more enjoyable.

John purchased The Vic in 2002, after working there for six years as cook, then server, then manager. His goal was to re-brand the traditional diner that it was and bring in a new attitude that encouraged the experience as much as it did food. He expanded the menu to include more upscale and creative cuisine that focused on fresh ingredients and flavor. He added a full bar that serves the Proud Mary, the ultimate Bloody Mary topped with shrimp, peperoncini, olive, cheese and a breadstick.

Today, The Vic serves more than 75,000 people each year in a space that sits just 40 guests.

hours we recommend going out of your early-day comfort zone and trying the Miscela Della Molla Salad with fresh mozzarella, pine nuts, Roma tomatoes and fresh basil, tossed with mesclun greens in a homemade balsamic vinaigrette and topped with a charbroiled chicken breast. The Victorian Club is also worth a lunch visit, with turkey, bacon, Roma tomatoes, avocado, and spring greens on thick sourdough with lemon aioli.

So go ahead, throw a big cheers John's way the next time you're hanging out with friends in front of the fire along Bend's warmest roundabout. The Vic, the Bend institution we now know, is all thanks to him.

FALLOW DEER EGGS BENEDICT

(Serves four)

1 lb Fallow deer sirloin

¼ cup fresh red peppers, diced small

1 cup fresh picked chanterelle mushrooms, sliced

¼ cup green onions, finely chopped

1 cup fresh ripe heirloom tomatoes, cut in wedges

4 homemade fresh cayenne chile biscuits (see recipe)

8 large eggs

1½ cups Fresh Sage Hollandaise Sauce (see recipe)

Cracked black pepper and salt

• Rub Fallow sirloin with fresh cracked pepper and salt then grill over medium/high heat just until rare. • Remove and slice ½ inch thick into four servings. • Begin poaching eggs and grilling biscuit halves until golden brown on one side. • At same time bring sauté pan to temperature and add chanterelles, peppers and onions. • When vegetables are hot add deer and then tomatoes. • Cook until deer is at desired temperature

(recommended medium rare). • Place two biscuit halves on each plate and top with equal amounts of deer and vegetable mixture. • Place a medium cooked poached egg over each half and top each with one ounce of sage hollandaise sauce. • Serve immediately.

FRESH SAGE HOLLANDAISE SAUCE

12 egg yolks

¼ cup white wine

1 Tbs Cholula hot sauce

¼ cup lemon Juice

1 lb melted butter

½ cup fresh chopped sage

Salt

• In a metal mixing bowl combine first four ingredients. • Whisk over medium heat until whisk shows clear tracks through mixture. • Remove from heat and slowly whisk in melted butter. • Add fresh sage and season to taste.

FRESH CAYENNE CHILE BISCUITS

(Makes 4 biscuits)

½ cup flour

1 tsp baking powder

½ tsp sugar

Pinch cream of tartar

Pinch salt

1-2 fresh cayenne chiles, sliced in thin rounds

2 Tbs shortening

2½ Tbs milk

• Mix first five ingredients together. • Cut in shortening until mixture resembles coarse crumbs. • Add milk all at once. Stir only until dough mixture follows fork around bowl. • Turn out on lightly floured surface. • Knead gently for 30 seconds. • Roll ½" thick then cut with biscuit cutter. • Bake on an ungreased baking sheet at 450° for 10 minutes.

BARRIO

A PAELLA PAN CAN BE A very powerful thing.

The epicenter of party, ceremony and debate, a paella pan carries history, flavor and a shape that nearly defines culture.

In the case of Steven Draheim, chef-owner of Barrio, a paella pan helped to seal the future of his brick-and-mortar restaurant.

While running his cult-followed food cart Soupcon alongside his friend and business partner Joel Cordes of El Sancho, the pair was approached with a can't-refuse opportunity to lease restaurant space on Minnesota Avenue in the heart of downtown Bend.

Amidst the normal process one goes through when deciding to open a restaurant, Steven thought about the antique paella pan he had purchased years before in Boise.

"Joel and I looked at each other and kind of thought, well, we have this giant paella pan… we might as well make use of it," laughed Steven.

With that, their lease was signed and Barrio was born.

Their concept? An eclectic, welcoming, neighborhood restaurant where sharing small, Latin-inspired dishes is affordable and approachable in the middle of a high-priced downtown dining scene.

They opened in March 2012, within a few weeks of signing the lease, on a mind-blowing budget of just $20,000. The big flavors produced in a tiny kitchen with heart and a great deal of street credit drew a loyal and enthusiastic crowd from day one.

Since that opening day, Barrio has served more than 50,000 tacos, been named "Rookie of the Year" restaurant by *The Source Weekly*, and become a one-owner operation. Joel, who is still a great friend of both Barrio and Steven and can sometimes be found poking his head in the kitchen, decided to part ways and continue running his El Sancho food cart.

Steven, a classically trained chef who has worked under James Beard award-winning chefs in Portland and Arizona, remains devoted to the restaurant and concept, although he misses the camaraderie that he and Joel shared in the kitchen.

"Ultimately, it's about everyone's happiness," said Steven. "But we're still evolving. We're still changing."

If you're joining Barrio for lunch, you'll want to look to the house chalkboard for a list of specials and fresh plates. At dinner, you can order several small tapas to share at the table with friends or select from the large platos menu where Shrimp, Eggplant & Manchego Tapas stands alongside a Barbacoa Lamb Chops. The Patatas Bravas, made with Yukon Gold potatoes, sofrito sauce and cotija cheese is a favorite on the tapas menu.

Four different types of paella fill the kitchen: House (chorizo and chicken), Mixta (House and seafood), Veggie & Seafood, and Vegetarian. There are two different sizes, small and large, in case you feel like sharing. The tacos are filled with carne asada, pork carnitas, grilled snapper, or mushroom and corn. The salads are fresh and seasonal and refresh with versions like the Grilled Salmon Caesar, made with crisp Romaine, grilled salmon, croutons, green chile dressing, lime and radish.

Much of the food is rice- and corn-based and heavily dependent on fresh vegetables, which makes vegetarians,

Have fun in your kitchen and support your local restaurants!

—Steven Draheim, chef-owner

vegans and anyone with gluten sensitivity feel right at home at Barrio.

And you'll want to order Sangria, a Barrio Margarita, or a Tamarind Whiskey Sour. Trust me.

No matter how you swing it at Barrio, you'll get consistent flavors of chile and lime that hit your pocket the right way.

"We try not to take ourselves too seriously. Barrio means neighborhood, but we're not a polished neighborhood," said Steven.

And in the end, that might be the most powerful characteristic of a well-worn paella pan. The longer it wears, the more scratches it gets, the more flavors it crisps, and the better it gets.

JERKED PORK TACOS
with Grilled Pineapple Salsa

(makes 24 tacos)

1   boneless pork shoulder, cut into large pieces

JERK PASTE

6   whole habanero peppers, stems removed
1   yellow onion, sliced into quarters
12 cloves garlic, peeled
    skin of 2 oranges
¾   cup orange juice
5   bay leaves
1   Tbs chopped, fresh thyme
12 whole allspice berries
½   cinnamon stick
1   Tbs brown sugar
½   cup fresh lime juice
½   cup olive oil
2   Tbs salt and pepper

• Lightly brown first three ingredients in a sauté pan with a small amount of oil.
• Combine all ingredients in a blender and blend on high for one minute, or until spices are ground.
• Marinate pork in the jerk paste overnight in the refrigerator.
• Caramelize pork in hot oil till brown and crispy on outside, should take about 15 minutes. • Brown each side evenly and then add chicken stock or water to come half way up the meat. • Cover and braise in a 400° oven for 2½ hours or until fork tender. • Strain the juices,

saving the liquid. • Spoon off grease from the liquid and set aside. • Shred pork with forks and add liquid back to the meat. Depending on how "wet" you want your meat, you may not need to add it all. • Hold warm while assembling the rest of the taco ingredients. • Feel free to add more jerk paste at this point.

GRILLED PINEAPPLE SALSA

1   pineapple, skin removed and cut around core in ½-inch sheets.
1   large red onion, cut into ½-inch thick rounds.
1   large jalapeño, grilled and finely chopped
¼   cup picked cilantro leaves
1   Tbs fresh lime juice
    Salt and pepper to taste

ADDITIONAL GARNISH

Avocado   Cabbage
White onion   Crema
Cotija cheese

• Grill pineapple, red onion and jalapeño till browned and grilled but not black.
• Small dice grilled ingredients and combine with cilantro, lime juice, salt and pepper.
• To assemble, we like to use two grilled tortillas per taco. Our favorite tortilla is a 5-inch corn tortilla from La Milpa in Sandy, Oregon. • Grill tortillas, place onto plate, however many you like, just keep two together. • Build your taco with jerked pork, pineapple salsa, fresh avocado, thinly sliced cabbage, chopped white onion, and crema or cotija cheese.

NOI THAI CUISINE

EVERY WEDNESDAY, A U-HAUL
truck pulls into the back alley behind Noi Thai Cuisine. Filled with 50-pound bags of Thai rice, coconut milk, spices, Thai dried chilles, noodles, straw mushrooms, bamboo shoots, and sweet basil—this is the moment that builds the flavorful base of downtown Bend's favorite Thai restaurant.

The team at Noi, spearheaded by head Chef Pag, is dedicated to serving authentic Thai food. So when that truck arrives each week, full of flavorful and exotic elements sourced from the best Thai suppliers, the Noi kitchen fills up as well, with a happy, happy Chef Pag.

"The owner, J.J., said to me before we opened, 'Don't worry if they are going to love it. Just give them real Thai food,'" said Chef Pag.

And with the support of owners J.J. Chaiseeha and his wife, Noi Lapangkura, along with general manager Sandy Burns, Chef Pag is doing just that.

Real Thai food, prepared on woks individually per order, floats through an elegant dining room where notes of Thai culture intrigue and enliven every guest that walks through the door. Two areas, dining room and lounge, are centered by a sunken well where floor-length curtains and a table set for six present special occasion dinners.

This is not a traditional, casual Thai restaurant, but rather a fine dining experience with a backdrop that is reminiscent of Bangkok in colors and textures and sheen and perfect for a

cocktail after work, dinner with friends or a lunch meeting.

Crispy Garlic Chicken, a Chef's Recommendation and referred to as "Chicken Crack" by most guests immediately after first taste, is by far the most popular plate. Juicy-on-the-inside, crispy-on-the-outside chicken pieces are stir-fried with a honey-infused mix of garlic and crisped sweet basil leaves. It all comes together for a sweet-salty-sour flavor that is intensely addictive.

The curries are timeless and classic. Red Curry is a favorite, featuring red chilles, lemongrass and shallots simmered with coconut milk, sweet basil, bamboo shoots, bell peppers and your choice of chicken, pork, beef or tofu.

Essential Heat

"If you want to cook Thai food, you have to control the temperature of your pan. You need a really hot pan. You must heat the pan before you put anything in it. And then move it all around while you cook!"

Chef Pag

The Green Curry emphasizes Kaffir lime peel and palm sugar. The Yellow Curry is the more mild selection with a hint of cumin and turmeric, coconut milk, potatoes and onions.

For most Noi diners, the moment of truth comes when deciding which rice to order. Jasmine, Coconut, Brown or Ginger? It's a unique and much-adored variety and many guests enjoy testing new combinations, although the standout favorites have always been Jasmine followed closely by Coconut.

For a chef that learned the basics of French cooking while studying in his birthplace of Thailand, Chef Pag admits it is a surprising thing to be cooking Thai food in America.

"In school, I never liked to cook Thai food. It was more exciting and cool to learn how the Europeans cook," said Chef Pag.

But one can conclude, after tasting his dishes and sensing the warm and true spirit of this young chef, that he eventually did grow a real passion for cooking authentic dishes of Thailand. Let's hope he continues to explore this cuisine, because we need more Crispy Garlic Chicken.

Photos Red Owl Photography

KHI MAO NOODLES

(Single serving)

This recipe is designed for a single serving because that is the traditional way to cook Thai food and the only way they cook dishes at Noi Thai Cuisine. If you are making for a larger party and do not have several pans to cook at once, you can double the recipe.

- 2 Tbs oil
- 6 oz chicken breast, thinly sliced
- 1 egg
- ½ tsp chopped garlic

- 3 broccoli florets
- 3 Tbs oyster sauce
- 5 Tbs soy sauce
- 1 Tbs fish sauce
- 2 tomato wedges
- 6 slices bell pepper (red or green)
- 10 basil leaves
  Thai chilles, chopped
- ¼ cup bamboo shoots
  Pinch of white pepper

• Put oil into hot wok and add chicken.

• Sauté slightly, add garlic and egg and stir until egg is cooked. • Add noodles and sauté lightly, keeping noodles separated from each other. • Add oyster sauce, soy sauce and fish sauce. • Stir into noodle mixture and add bell peppers, broccoli, bamboo shoots and simmer for about one minute. • Add tomato, basil and white pepper. Stir-fry until basil has softened but not turned black. • Add Thai chilles to your liking.

THE HIDEAWAY TAVERN

🍴 IF YOU KNOW JOHN NOLAN, owner of both The Victorian Café (see page 110) and The Hideaway Tavern, you know that he is a game guy. With two game rooms at home and a large social circle, he's not shy about having friends over for football and hockey nights.

Several years ago though, he got to thinking: where in Bend do you go to watch a game and eat really good, healthy food? (Besides his house.) Where do you go to catch your favorite team or sport, without feeling like you need to be part of a certain group?

The Hideaway Tavern is the sports bar that John always wanted to see in Bend. All the favorites of a typical sports bar—18 beers (mostly local microbrews) on tap, 8 flat screen TVs, a pool table, leather couches, darts, foosball, house ground burgers, hand-tossed pizzas, truffle mac & cheese, poutine, a prime rib grinder — but, wait, this is not your typical sports bar.

"The Vic is my kitchen. The Hideaway is my living room," said John.

With better food, better sports, and certainly better times, this is one of the best living rooms we've seen in Bend.

Open for lunch and dinner during the week and

breakfast, lunch and dinner on the weekends, you can pretty much walk into The Hideaway at any time and be assured you're going to be welcomed, well-fed and entertained.

In addition to the upscale sports bar food, you'll also find old favorites like the Buffalo Drumsticks. Reminiscent of the classic hot wing, but better, the drumsticks are first smoked, then fried, sautéed and baked, and served with a house-made blue cheese. The Stuffed Jalapeños summon memories of poppers but, again, better because of a bacon-wrapped exterior and stuffing that's made with homemade pork and cheddar sausage.

If you love sports, but err on the side of lighter game fare, The Hideaway is also a place for you. Salads, including The Mother Grain, filled with red quinoa and wheatberry, and Brussels Baby with shaved sprouts, baby kales and toasted pine nuts, are fresh, vegetarian alternatives to typical bar food.

The weekend breakfast is a relatively new addition to the mix. Hit The Hideaway on Saturday and Sunday morning for a Game Changer Bloody Mary and Cinnamon Twist French Toast, Classic Eggs Benedict, Wild Steelhead Benedict, Carnitas Egg Chimichanga, or Granola with fruit and yogurt while you catch the early east coast football games.

John is a hockey player, so whether it's early season or the middle of playoffs, hockey is an important sport at The Hideaway. Tuesday and Thursday nights garner a group of passionate NHL fans. And while John notes that "football is definitely king," you can watch any sport you want on the flat screens that fill the walls. Soccer? Baseball? Golf? America's Cup? The Hideaway has it all.

They serve multiple variations of the poutine, a Canadian dish made with French fries, topped with gravy and cheese curds. The Hideaway version is Braised Duck Poutine with Fresh Mozzarella Curd. It's a dish that really sums it up. This is a sports bar for everyone.

Party Time

Prepare as much as you can ahead of time. I don't want to be taken out of the party. I want to be in the party!

—John Nolan, owner

BRAISED DUCK POUTINE
With Fresh Mozzarella Curd

(Serves 4-6)

You can easily make the Mozzarella Curd and Duck Gravy in advance. On the day of serving, heat the gravy while the fries are cooking and then assemble. Voila! You have an easy, carefree dish that will seriously impress your friends on game day.

MOZZARELLA CURD

1   lb fresh mozzarella curd
2   cups of kosher salt
3   quarts of water

• In a 4-quart pot, bring water and salt to a boil.

• In a large mixing bowl, shred mozzarella curd into small chunks roughly the size of grapes.

• Set a large ice bath.

• Pour boiling water over the shredded mozzarella curd and let it stand for 7 minutes, then pour off excess water until there is roughly 2 inches of water over the curd.

• Submerge hands into ice bath, then with a wooden spoon, scoop out melted curd in small amounts, while continually stretching and folding the cheese over the spoon until it reaches a smooth consistency. • Once that is accomplished remove the curd from the spoon and form into a ball and place it into the ice bath. • When cooled remove from ice bath and strain off excess water.

DUCK GRAVY

5   lbs duck thighs
1   qt chicken stock
1   Tbs red pepper flakes
2   Tbs chopped Italian parsley
1   Tbs kosher salt
1   cup roux
¼   cup of chopped green onions
¼   cup of fresh grated Grana cheese
4   servings of fresh cut French fries

• Preheat oven to 375°

• In a shallow baking dish place duck thighs with ½ inch of water in the bottom. • Add salt and pepper to the exposed duck, cover and for 45 minutes or longer, braise until it pulls easily off of the bone.

• In a saucepot over medium-high heat add chicken stock, salt, and red pepper flakes and begin to reduce.

• Once the duck meat is pulled off the bone, add it to your sauce and simmer ingredients for 20 minutes until the duck begins to shred.

• Slowly begin whisking the roux into your gravy until you get the consistency desired. (See page 46 for tips from EaT: An Oyster Bar on making great roux.)

SERVING

French fries cooking method is your choice. • Cook fries until they are ¾ of the way done. • Place desired serving amounts over parchment paper on an ungreased cookie sheet.

• Shred mozzarella balls into small chunks over the top of the servings of fries then place cookie sheets into your pre-heated oven. • Bake until the mozzarella begins to melt.

• Remove from oven, and place the portion of fries still on the parchment paper on plates. • Put equal amounts of gravy on each serving. • Garnish with grated Grana cheese and green onions.
• Serve immediately.

Photos Douglas Miller

BELLATAZZA

🍴 DOWNTOWN BEND AND SUNRIVER
– Brilliant, simple coffee built on the finest traditions from Yemen, Mexico City and Paris. A perfectly extracted espresso with 1 oz of milk. Big, bold flavors, but not expensive price tags. A Guatemalan roast that sings with its

history, its community, its humanity. An iced toddy that's cold-brewed for ten hours and needs nothing but a simple glass and glistening rocks. Friends from all walks of life that meet over coffee and politics, music and art, theatre and life. A soundtrack of Cuban, New York down-tempo, minimal techno. Roasted Ethiopian beans that roast well before dark, doing the bean absolute justice. Baristas that bring a vibrant spirit and youthful idealism to each cup and interaction. Pastries from passionate local bakeries. Milk from the local dairy.

Everything about Bellatazza, a coffee house and roaster in downtown Bend and Sunriver, oozes java knowledge, authentic cool and local-brewed spirit.

This vibe comes straight from the top, from owner Stewart Fritchman who has been learning, living and loving coffee for most of his

A Vintage European Coffee Van Hits the Streets of Bend

It's hard to miss the Bellatazza coffee van. Shiny silver, angular, trimmed in bright orange—it's somewhat of an icon in Bend, even though this mobile unit is still a newbie on the scene. You can't pass this van and not smile. It's like a chic ice cream truck for the big kids.

The 1970 Citroen H came to Bellatazza by way of Europe. After a long search, it was

found northwest of Paris, covered in bat guano, owl pellets and resident Parisian felines—a scene straight out of Disney's Ratatouille. Despite its dire neglect, the vintage van had potential and was exactly what Bellatazza owner Fritchman was looking for. So he found restoration experts and completely reclaimed its beautiful spirit, a process that took nearly two years. The van can now be found at local events around town serving up Bellatazza coffee on the go.

life. He remembers being drawn to his parents' whole bean grinder as a child and climbing up on the kitchen counter just to get a whiff of the freshly pulsed beans.

As a college student in Seattle, he nurtured a love affair with coffee culture, spending most of his off-time in coffee shops. "I started to notice that a coffee house is the only place in the world where everyone comes in on solid, equal ground," he said.

Transfixed with this idea, Fritchman started learning the art of coffee making and purchased his first coffee venture in 1991, an espresso cart in Portland he named Kiosk. He says he didn't know much at the time, but as a hungry student he fell in love quickly with learning the art and merging it with his interest in Mayan culture and a strong internal pull to Latin America. Step by step, he learned about process, quality, business, roasting and global relationships that extend beyond the cup. Eventually he found himself in Central Oregon and opened Bellatazza in Sunriver (formerly the Sunriver Coffee Company) in 1996 and a second shop in downtown Bend in 2002.

Bellatazza in Bend is a hub of downtown spirit. On any given afternoon you can find artists, street musicians, break dancers, old men reading the newspaper, college students adorned with laptops and headphones, or tourists sitting on the front patio drinking coffee and watching the world go by. It is a welcoming place, a diverse place, an epicenter of conversation and community, which is exactly as Stewart envisioned it to be.

RECIPE FOR A MIND-BLOWING CUP

Bellatazza owner Stewart Fritchman figures he's visited more than 500 coffee shops around the globe. He has also made it a personal goal ,while out of the United States, to make coffee in every café he steps foot in. Self-taught in Spanish, he works his way behind the counter and asks "Can I make?" This is part of his never-ending learning process, and also reflects the very nature of a man that lives life in pursuit of community. A man who, when asked about his favorite bottle of wine, does not recount a label or region or year, but rather the people he shared it with, the conversations it helped manifest, and whether they had so much fun they howled at the moon .

So, despite tasting coffee in celebrated and obscure houses around the world, it was a single cup of coffee in a small Guatemalan village that forever left a mark on his palate.

He was in Panajachel, a village in the southwestern Guatemalan Highlands, at the home of Rosa, a young woman whom Stewart had met at market while she was selling her fabric to tourists. Stewart learned about Rosa's life, and keeping in step with his allure for Latin America and Direct Trade relationships with micro coffee plantations in the area, decided to sponsor Rosa and her family. One day, while at her home, Rosa's sister offered to make him a cup of coffee. She roasted beans on a humble stovetop and ground them by hand on a traditional mortar and pestle table that dated 300 years.

There was no talk about flavor profiles and acidity levels that

Photos Jill Rosell Photography

day. That cup, that experience, that community, that history, was about family and story and connection. And that, to Fritchman, is essential to brewing a mind-blowing cup of coffee.

Photos Russ McIntosh of Studio Absolute

CAFÉ SINTRA

"I'VE WORKED THIS CORNER FOR most of my life," laughed Tracie Landsem, owner of Sunriver's Café Sintra.

This corner being the corner of Ponderosa Road, where Central Oregon's most popular Portuguese café found its home in The Village at Sunriver.

Forty years ago though, this corner housed Tree House Pizza Parlor, where Tracie began her restaurant career at the age of 15. She delivered pizza and fried chicken to hungry vacationers and for the first time in her life began to pay close attention to the kitchen.

When Tree House closed and was sold to Marcello's, Tracie stayed. She began to cook Italian cuisine and learn the fine art of pasta making, baking and wine service.

"I really grew up at Marcello's," said Tracie.

Through these years, she got to know the regular vacation crowd in the small resort community of Sunriver and watched children grow and parents become grandparents. She knew many of them by name and would even call and check up on some of them if they didn't come around for a while.

When the opportunity arose to help open Café Sintra in Sunriver, Tracie jumped on it. She didn't have to go far. It was opening in the very same corner building, just next to Marcello's.

Named after the town of Sintra in Portugal, Café Sintra is open for breakfast and lunch and specializes in delicious breakfast and lunch dishes that pay tribute to Portuguese cuisine. The warm atmosphere and the friendly service makes Café Sintra the perfect place for gatherings and a nice stop for a good espresso drink and homemade pastries.

Portuguese cuisine is notable for its bold use of herbs and spices. The ever-popular Portuguese sausage linguiça combines mild seasonings such as garlic, onions, salt, oregano and paprika. At Café Sintra, this sausage is paired with sautéed onions, sweet peppers, mushrooms and herb mayonnaise for a flavorful lunch sandwich. You can also find it in a Pizzetta, the Sintra con Carne Tacos, the Sintra Benedict (an absolute favorite), and a breakfast egg scramble with sautéed onions, mushrooms and fresh cilantro.

> *"I always say, cooking, it has to come from the heart."*
>
> –Tracie Landsem, owner

The breads and pastries are mostly Tracie's recipes and they are all homemade. Scones, croissants, linguiça biscuits, Pastel de Nata (an egg custard pastry), muffins and apple cinnamon twists are all made with homemade dough, high-quality ingredients, and a love that can only come from scratch.

"I always say that cooking has to come from the heart," said Tracie. "The more love you put into it, the more it shows you care, the better the food tastes."

The pancakes, also made from scratch, are delectable. Light, airy, slightly sweet and perfectly golden, they are as much enjoyed by adults as by children. Topped with just a

SUNRIVER

slight dusting of powdered sugar and fresh berries, they are a delightful way to start any day and go perfectly with an expert espresso drink.

"Sometimes, I'm at the espresso machine making a latte and look out the door to a line of fifty people waiting," said Tracie. "But in that moment, I center, and find happiness in taking my time and making the very best latte."

These are the words of someone with a long history in the restaurant business. Someone who has a loyal following of happy guests and diners. Someone who found her place, several decades ago, on one small corner in Sunriver.

Bean Basics

For Café Sintra's Portuguese Stew, you can substitute canned beans for dried beans if you must, but dried beans are so much better tasting and better for you. The process is not difficult.

Clean your beans Spread dry beans in a single layer on a large sheet tray. Pick through to remove and discard any small stones or debris. Rinse well.

Soak your beans In a large bowl, cover beans with cold water 3 inches above top of beans. Cover and set aside at room temperature for 8 hours or overnight. If you're in a rush, you can cover with cold water, cover and boil for 1 minute. Then remove from heat and set aside, covered, for 1 hour.

Use your beans Dump beans into a colander and rinse with cold water. Use in any recipe calling for beans.

PORTUGUESE STEW

(Makes 6-8 Bowls)

This is a family recipe of Manuel dos Santos, owner of Café Sintra in downtown Bend. He named the restaurant after his hometown in Portugal, near Lisbon. This popular stew was adapted from his grandmother's recipe. It can be found in both locations of the café and is available every day.

2	lbs dry white beans
1	Tbs salt
2	cups chicken stock
1	whole chicken, boiled
2	cups chicken broth, reserved from boiling
1	onion, diced
1	small can of green chiles
2	Tbs olive oil
1	tsp cumin
	Sour cream for garnish
	Cilantro for garnish
	Sliced green apples for garnish

- Clean and soak beans overnight.
- Drain and rinse.

- Boil the beans in plenty of water with salt until tender. • Drain completely, reserving some of the water.

- In a separate pot, boil chicken.
- Cook until meat is cooked through and tender. • Set aside to cool, reserving the broth. • Cut chicken into small pieces and strips, discarding skin once cooled. • Skim the top of the broth and discard fat.

- In another pot, fry onions in olive oil until golden. • Add green chiles, chicken and cumin. • Add 2 cups chicken stock and 2 cups of reserved broth. • Add the white beans and water.

- Let simmer for 30 minutes.

- Serve hot and top with sour cream, sliced apples and cilantro.

SUNRIVER

ABOUT TEAM SIZZLE & BUZZ

JOHN HERBIK
Founder & President

John started The Where to Eat Guide & Associates, Inc in Bend, Oregon in 2005. A veteran sales and marketing professional, John also has extensive experience in the restaurant and hospitality industry. It was his passion for both that drove him to create a magazine that is now the premier vehicle for restaurant promotion in the Pacific Northwest.

SARAH DAILY
Writer

Although she spends most of her professional time on social media marketing, publicity and public relations projects for her clients, Sarah will always consider herself a writer at heart. With a degree in journalism, she is a listener of stories, and is at more attention when those stories are told in a warm, aroma-filled kitchen with great food, great wine and a passionate cook.

DANA BARTUS
Creative Director &
Personal Assistant to John Herbik

A true Jersey girl, Dana is still learning the west coast ways. She has over 10 years of experience in the restaurant industry, a background of graphic design and fine art, and a passion for travel and experiencing the unknown. She recently joined The Where to Eat Guide & Associates, Inc. by chance, or more specifically, by way of yoga. Her organization skills, project management and creative direction were key to the execution of *Sizzle & Buzz*.

Michaele Grabenhorst

SALLY SUNDSTEN
Production & Graphic Designer

A "native Oregonian since 1972," Sally got her start in graphic design back when newspapers literally cut and pasted clip art and type on page layouts. Moving from newspapers to commercial printing opened doors wide and she now has clients for everything from business cards to brochures to books. Recruited to help launch *The Where To Eat Guide* in Bend, she has enjoyed being a part of the evolution and growth of the company.

Natasha Ray

JASON STAATS
Pacific Northwest Director of Sales

A native Oregonian, Jason is one of the brightest personalities in Portland. He is a strong force in the hospitality field, always supporting small business with his savvy hotel concierge background and passion for the restaurant industry. Jason was recruited for a sales position with *The Where to Eat Guide* in 2010 and continues to excel in the areas of regional sales and company development. In his off time, he enjoys driving his 1973 Super Beetle named Sunny, gluten-free beer and dinner parties with family and friends.

ACKNOWLEDGEMENTS

The Where to Eat Guide & Associates, Inc. would like to thank John Furguson for his friendship and insight on branding and marketing, for his choice of title and tagline, as well as his ongoing support of *The Where To Eat Guide* magazine; Aaron Fry for his contribution of cover art design and creativity; Jason Staats for his efforts in keeping all the balls in the air while we produced this book; Sally Sundsten for her ongoing work with the magazine, her ability to handle stress and deadlines has been key in keeping everything running over the past 8 years; Sarah Daily for all the invisible work that went into writing this book, for maintaining our social media presence through Facebook pages, and all the press release work necessary in promoting *Sizzle & Buzz*; Dana Bartus for coming through when John needed her most; Jill Mowlds for proofing and editing this book, and her ongoing support of the magazines over the years; Amy Voeller and Randy Rolphe for their consistency as the best practiced print wholesalers in the region; Stephanie Tastad for her legwork with charities and face time on local television, along with the promotional Twitter push (follow her @WTEGgirlSEATTLE); Matthew Finfer for his knowledge and skills in handling the additional workload; Ryan Comingdeer and Five Talent Software for keeping us up on the web; William Durden for his writing knowledge and proofreading skills; J.C. Nore for his printing research; Michael Harris for encouraging us to put this book together after he completed his first book *Falling Down and Getting Up*; John's son, Zach, for his patience and sacrifice over the years while John launched the magazine with a nearly 24/7 work-minded lifestyle, for his willingness to help ensure that the business continues to run properly, for distribution, and client correspondence with hotels and front desk concierge; Melissa for her support in managing Zach and his dog, Cookie's time while John traveled to launch the magazines all the way through publishing our first book; friends and family for all their encouragement and positive support.

Special thanks to all the restaurants who have participated with *The Where To Eat Guide* over the years, thank you, thank you, thank you. Without you, we would not have been able to put together and maintain the premier dining guide and #1 tool used by the best hotels in all our markets.

PHOTOGRAPHERS

All photography copyrights reserved to the individual photographers.
All restaurants are credited for providing the images that are not listed.

Alison Jones of the Screen Door 50
Ariel Dawn Photography 96, 97
Barbour, Lincoln 32, 33
Boyd, Thomas 36
Brock, Peter 40
Buchanan, Deborah 48, 49
Castano, Amy 92, 108, 109
Chris Jordan of Shipwreck Design 84, 85
Fenske, Jeremy 34
Granen, John 60, 61
Garling, Ellie 106
Halterman, Julie 105
Heeb, Christian 92
Henry, Michael 81
Holdsworth, Joe 76, 77
Holmboe, Nick 34
Jill Rosell Photography 118, 119
Lange-Scoval, Mesa 41
Lybeck, Katie 80

Maclartn, Troy 35
Miller, Douglas 110, 111, 116, 117
Nicole Hart Photography 45
Over, Eric 86, 87
Parsons, Tim 18, 19
Patrick, Juliana 40
Peterson, Bob 90, 91, 125
Ray, Natasha 122
Reamer, David 6, 8, 12, 13, 16, 17
Ribary, Ryan 20, 21
Robichaud, Tyson 26, 27
Russ McIntosh of Studio Absolute
    6, 120, 121
Schafer, Rich 24, 25
Smith, Geoffrey 82, 83
Staats, Jason 46, 54, 55, 88, 89
Taylor, Rachell 70, 71
Tiffany Lausen of Red Owl Photography
    100-103, 114, 115

Table of Contents: Page 4 - UR - Dan &
    Louis Oyster Bar; LL - Smallwares;
    Page 5 - UR - Lowell's; LL - Barrio
Index: Page 124 - Tabla; Page 125 - Bob
    Peterson; Page 127 – Jodi Porad

PHOTO MONTAGES
Page 6: UL - Davis Street Tavern; ML -
    Serratto; UR - Russ McIntosh of Studio
    Absolute; MR - David Reamer; LL -
    Laurelhurst Market; LR - Matt's in the
    Market
Page 8: UR - David Reamer; ML - Delicatus;
    LL - Bollywood; LR - Serratto
Page 10: ML - Parish; MR - Cafe Nell;
    LL - Davis Street Tavern; LR - Wildwood
Page 58: ML - Row House; MR - Lowell's;
    LL - Hunger 2.0
Page 92: Upper - ©Christian Heeb/
    ccophotostock.com; ML - Amy
    Castano; MR - Brickhouse; LL - Chow;
    LR - Barrio

INDEX

Bob Peterson

CONTINUED ON NEXT PAGE

THE WHERE TO EAT GUIDE

THANKS FOR YOUR SUPPORT

The purchase of this book will benefit the following charities in the Pacific Northwest

Operation Sac Lunch:
http://www.oslserves.org

Portland Police Bureau's Sunshine Division:
http://www.sunshinedivision.org

The Hunger Prevention Coalition of Central Oregon:
http://www.hungerpc.org

Jodi Porad

CHEFS

OWNER / OPERATORS